THE MICHIGAN FUR TRADE

BY

IDA AMANDA JOHNSON

THE BLACK LETTER PRESS
Grand Rapids
1971

 BLACK LETTER PRESS
1201 Butler, S.E.
Grand Rapids, Mich. 49507

9.95 U.S. JAN '80

First Published 1919 by the Michigan Historical Commission

Authorized Reprinting 1971 by the Black Letter Press

Second Reprinting 1975 By Black Letter Press

Library of Congress Catalogue Card Number: 74-155928

PRINTED IN THE UNITED STATES OF AMERICA

PREFACE

THIS little study aims to give an account of the fur trader's régime in Michigan; to show the trading policy of the various nations which successively held sway over her territory and its results, and the gradual transition from the influence and domination of one government to that of another; to relate the story of the rise and growth of the various posts and outposts within Michigan's borders, the influences to which they were subjected and their fortunes in peace and war; to depict the life of the traders, their relations to the red men and to each other; and finally, to show what place these forest rovers, the frontier heroes of the State, hold in her history.

I wish to thank all private citizens, officers of historical societies, and librarians who have kindly assisted me in obtaining material sought. I am especially indebted to Mr. Clarence M. Burton of Detroit, who generously permitted me to use his large and valuable collection of manuscripts and books on the history of the Northwest. To Professor C. H. Van Tyne of the University of Michigan, at whose suggestion this work was undertaken, I wish to express my sincere thanks for the kind suggestions and helpful criticisms given while the work was in progress.

PREFACE TO SECOND EDITION

Since the publication of Ida Johnson's *Michigan Fur Trade* in 1919, new manuscripts have been located, and hundreds of books and articles about the fur trade have been published. Two general works that contain detailed bibliographies are Harold Innis, *The Fur Trade in Canada* (New Haven: Yale University Press, 1930), and Paul C. Phillips, *The Fur Trade* (Norman: University of Oklahoma Press, 1961). Milo Quaife edited two volumes of the *John Askin Papers* (Detroit: Detroit Library Commission, 1928, 1931), essential for research in the entire Great Lakes region.

The most unusual study of recent years is by Lewis O. Saum, *The Fur Trader and the Indian* (Seattle: University of Washington Press, 1965), which presents the Indian point of view. The *Rapports de l'Archiviste de la Province de Quebec*, published annually since 1921, contain lists of all trade permits issued to Great Lakes traders during the French and British regimes. Since 1966, two volumes of the *Dictionary of Canadian Biography* have appeared, containing entries for such individuals as Radisson, Cadillac, Legardeur de St. Pierre, and Jolliet.

During the past few decades the best interpretive works on fur trade have appeared in state historical quarterlies. For example, the winter, 1966, issue of *Minnesota History* contains nine articles that were originally presented at the 1965 North American Fur Trade Conference. The fall, 1967, issue of *Michigan History* is devoted to frontier missions, 1812-1850. The focus in the articles is on the role of the missionary in an economy shifting from the fur trade to farming, lumbering, and mining.

Although the recent fur trade literature is extensive, no author has attempted to summarize the entire fur trade epoch as Ida Johnson did in her 1919 work. Gaps remain in her survey, and some of her interpretations are questionable. Yet, when used with more recent sources, the *Michigan Fur Trade* can be a valuable research tool.

Donald Chaput
Michigan Historical Commission

CONTENTS

French Régime, 1634-1760

CHAPTER I

PIONEER TRADE................. 1

Introduction
How Michigan was favored for fur trade
  Her geographical position
  Her furred animals
Her fur trade régimes
French policy of trade
  Colonizing companies
  License system
Pioneer traders
  Jean Nicolet
  The coureurs de bois
  Groseilliers and Radisson
  La Salle
  The Jesuits and their relation to trade
Early posts of trade during the French régime
  Sault Ste. Marie
    Early visits
    Abandonment
  Michilimackinac
    Its importance
    English luring Indians and traders from the post
    Coming of Flemish and English
  Founding of Fort St. Joseph by DuLhut
Effort to centralize Michigan trade
Intercolonial wars and their effect on Michigan trade
Trade in St. Joseph Valley
Fur prices and amount of fur in the seventeenth century
The liquor traffic and trade
  Early attempts to check it
  How liquor laws were evaded
Illicit trade
  Results
  Licenses revoked and all traders recalled from the
    Upper Country, particularly from Michilimackinac
Conditions of trade at the close of the seventeenth century

CHAPTER II

DETROIT THE GREAT DEPOT OF TRADE........ 31

Reason for its founding
  Key point for checking English and Iroquois advance
  Cadillac anxious to locate there
  Variety of furred animals in its environs
Its enemies
  Iroquois
  French officials
  Jesuits
Periods of its trading career
  Under the company
    Their policy
    Effort to suppress the beaver hunt
    Failure of company
  Under Cadillac
    Drawing of savage tribes to Detroit
    Cadillac and the liquor traffic
    Illicit trade
    Inhabitants and trade
    Cadillac removed and sent to Louisiana
  Under various rulers
    The régime of Sir de La Forest
    The régime of M. de Sabrevois
    The régime of Alphonse de Tonty
    The régime of Sieur de Noishebert
Unrest among the Indians causes decline in trade
The independent trader

CHAPTER III

REVIVAL OF MICHILIMACKINAC AND OTHER POSTS....52

The effect of Detroit's establishment on Michilimackinac
Michilimackinac at the opening of the eighteenth century
Michilimackinac the stopping place of *coureurs de bois*
Michilimackinac re-established
  Licenses restored
  Chief Indian tribes trading there
  Slowly regains her former trading position
  Effect of Intercolonial war on the posts
  Outposts of

Sault Ste. Marie
  Re-establishment by Repentigny
St. Joseph Valley
  Military fort on river
  Indians trading there
  British intrigues
  Post farmed out
Passing of French régime

British Régime, 1760-97

CHAPTER IV

BRITISH POLICY AND EARLY TRADE........ 64

British policy of trade
  Its free policy
  Presents for the Indians
  Abandonment of useless posts
Comparison of French and British policy
English take possession of Detroit
English take possession of Michilimackinac
The English pioneer trader at Michilimackinac
  His disguise
  Discovered and visited by Chippeways
  The Ottawas arrive and demand goods on credit
  Henry and companions in danger
    Saved by Lieutenant Leslie
Sault Ste. Marie and St. Joseph in the early days
English traders' fear of the Indians
The extent of their trade
Pontiac's War and its effect on Michigan trade
Michilimackinac after the war
  Henry gets the exclusive trade of the Lake Superior
    region
Detroit
  Indian nations solicit trade
  Traders have upper hand
Sault Ste. Marie
English officials' attitude towards trade
Character of this pre-revolutionary period of trade

CHAPTER V

Michigan Fur Trade in Revolutionary Times.   78

Phases of the period considered
The effect of war upon Michigan trade
    Unrest among the Indians
    Hindrance to transportation
        Means of transportation in early days
            The canoe
            The trading vessel
            Kings' orders against sailing of private vessels
            John Askin's activity in forwarding supplies for
                traders
            Attempts to solve the problem of getting
                supplies
Competitive war among traders
    The character of the competition
        The use of liquor
        Other means
        Result of contest
Forming of Michilimackinac Association of 1779
    Terms of agreement
    Their interests on the river St. Joseph
    Failure of the concern
Another effort at union
Formation of the North West Company
    Early agreements
    Permanent organization
Mackinac Company
    Its relation to Michigan trade
Character of the new trading contest
The Independent trader
Character of fur trade at Detroit at this time
The Michilimackinac trader
Sault Ste. Marie
St. Joseph Valley
        Location of the Le Claires
Minor posts established in this period
Amount of furs collected
Kind of furs handled

Entrance of American influence
    The American trader Burnette
    Efforts of English to check his trade
    English fear the loss of trade in American territory
        Their petition

The American Régime, 1796-1840

CHAPTER VI

U. S. POLICY AND THE EXTENSION OF ITS TRADE INTO MICH-
            IGAN.....................   102

Character of American régime
American fur-trade policy
    The factory system
    The license system
    Instructions given to licensed trader
A brief survey of entire régime
Michigan posts pass into United States' hands
American influence transplants that of the English
    Through the influx of traders
    Through establishment of government factories
        At Detroit
        At Michilimackinac
    Through rise of Astor's fur-trading company
Astor secures a share in the Mackinac company
Sault Ste. Marie
    British desire to hold
    Dispute between two rival companies over the control
        of the strait
Growing hostility between English and American traders
    British smuggling goods for trading purposes
    Firing on the Mackinac convoy by American soldiers
    Grievances of American trader
Conditions of trade

CHAPTER VII

Trade During the War of 1812 and Early Operations of the American Fur Company.......... 117

Capture of Michilimackinac by the English
  Effect upon Astor
  Ramsey Crooks' efforts to carry on trade at that place
Transportation hindered by war
  Carrying of private goods on the lakes forbidden
    Effect upon trade
  Astor secures temporary suspension of rule
  Goods of The South West and other British firms removed
Effect of war on the trade at the Sault
  John Johnston's property destroyed
  Property of the North West Company destroyed
  Their furs from the interior pass
Detroit trade during the war
  Perry's treaty with the Indians
  Crooks' attempt to trade there futile
Effects of the war on the fortunes of the American Fur Company
The disappearance of the North Westers
Early days of the American Fur Company
  Foreigners forbidden to trade within the United States
  Operations directly after the war
  Organization of the Lake Superior trade
  Traders of the company
  Regions of trade

CHAPTER VIII

Michigan Fur Trade at Its Height...... 127

Michigan trading conditions in 1816
"Oppositions" in trade
Michigan's main regions of trade
  Grand River Valley traders
    Madame La Framboise
    Rix Robinson
    Louis Campau
    Detroit representatives
    Other traders

Saginaw traders
    Contest between Louis Campau and American
        Fur Company's agent
    Abbott Bros.
    Williams Bros.
    The "Shiawassee Exchange"
    Other traders
Posts scattered through the interior
Old entreports of trade
    Sault Ste. Marie
    St. Joseph Valley
    Detroit
    Michilimackinac

CHAPTER IX

The Closing Days of the Michigan Fur Trade.   146

The United States factory system abolished
    Opposition to it
    Causes of its failure
Hostility to prevailing license system
    The system abused
Attitude of American traders to settlers
    Attitude of their predecessors
    Change of spirit
    Indians give up their hunting grounds in Michigan
Liquor traffic during the American régime
    Indians confiscate liquor illegally brought into their
        country
    Difficulty of controlling liquor traffic when settlers
        enter
Decline of fur trade at Detroit
J. B. Hubbel buys property of American Fur Company at
    Michilimackinac
Michigan fur-trading posts disappear

CHAPTER X

The Trader's Life..............   154

Character of the life they led
Various classes of traders
    Coureurs de bois

Bourgeois
Partisan
Voyageur
Mangeurs de lard
Clerk
Hivernans or winterers
Artisans
Free trapper
Character of the fur traders
Their relation to the Indian
Their food
Difficulties of securing
Their places of rest
Their recreation
Indian story-telling
Revels and feasts at the great trading marts
Method of trade
Crossing the portages
Outfits
Summary of the history of the Michigan fur trade

Appendix 181
Bibliography 185
Index 196

THE MICHIGAN FUR TRADE

The French Régime, 1634-1760

CHAPTER I

PIONEER TRADE

MICHIGAN played a prominent role in the early fur-trading régime of the great Northwest. For over two centuries[1] the trader in pelts, that forerunner and scout of the civilized commonwealth, reigned practically supreme within her domain, and it was not until the emigrant and settler deprived the Indian of his hunting ground that her fur-trading folk disappeared.

Two things contributed toward making her a leading section in the early fur trade. The first, and no doubt the most potent factor, was her location; the second, her abundant supply of fur-bearing animals.

Michigan by her very position was destined to become an important trading section, for her routes of travel in pioneer days were largely the waterways; she lay in the very heart of the Great Lakes region, her shores washed by the four lakes, Erie, Huron, Michigan and Superior. Her territory was cut in twain by the Straits of Mackinac, which formed a

1. From 1634 to 1840-50.

link in the chain of waterways connecting the East
with the Mississippi and its tributaries and which for
a long time was the highway by which the French
and all the Nations of the South were obliged to pass
in going to and returning from Montreal.[2] Fearing
the powerful Iroquois on the south, they took what
was known as the upper route to the Northwest, i. e.,
from Montreal up the Ottawa River, across by land
to Lake Nipissing and down the French River to
Georgian Bay.[3] From there, these little trading crews
crossed Lake Huron. The Straits of Mackinac gave
them entrance to Lake Michigan, over which they
passed to Wisconsin and Illinois, and from there to
the trading posts on the Mississippi and her eastern
tributaries.[4] The latter were for many years the
frontier posts of trade, sending their furs to and seeking
their goods of exchange from Montreal. Michigan,
in a central location as to these sources of supply
and demand, through whose very territory furs and
merchandise had to be carried, naturally became a
middle ground where the supplies of the East were
exchanged for the rich peltries of the West. A narrow
waterway on her eastern shore connected Lake Huron
with Lake Superior, making it possible to extend the
early trade far westward toward the center of the

2. Margry, *Déc. et étab.*, V, 67.
3. *Wis. Hist. Colls.*, XVIII, 144; Sheldon, *Hist. of Mich.*, 39.
    Numerous instances of Iroquois attack upon the French
    are told in the *Jesuit Relations*.
4. There were two routes by which the Mississippi was reached
    from Lake Michigan; one by way of Green Bay and the
    Fox and Wisconsin; the other by way of the Lake to
    Chicago River. Wis. Hist. Society *Proceedings*, 1889,
    p. 58.

continent;[5] and, just as Sault Ste. Marie was in early days spoken of as the key and door to the Nations of the north who wished to visit the French settlements,[6] and as Mackinaw became the great mart of exchange for the west and southwest, so Detroit held the key to the upper-country trade for those south and southeast of that point.

Not only did her geographical position favor Michigan for the fur trade; her forests were teeming with fur-bearing animals whose pelts would for many years have richly supplied her little trading posts and given her a place in the history of this important branch of commerce.[7]

As Michigan passed successively under the dominion

5. Turner tells how the early traders, choosing to go from Huron Island through Sault Ste. Marie into Lake Superior, were forced to hug the shore because of their frail canoes, and rumors of copper mines induced them to take the southern shore. Wis. Hist. Society *Proceedings*, 1889, p. 58.

6. *Jes. Rel.*, LV, 97, 157.

7. Cadillac mentions the following as being found near Detroit: elks, moose, wolves, bears, otters, lynxes, beavers, muskrats. *Mich. Hist. Colls.*, XXXIII, 135, 144, 200.

"From the earliest times St. Clair Co. was noted for its beaver. La Hontan who spent part of 1687-8 at Ft. St. Joseph (Du Lhut's fort) at the entrance of the river St. Clair, produced a map attached to a book published by him in 1790. On this map near Ft. St. Joseph are these words: 'Beaver hunting of the friends of the French.'"—Jenks, *Hist. of St. Clair Co.*, I, 45.

In the St. Joseph Valley, besides the buffalo were found the bear, the elk, the deer, beaver, otter, martin, raccoon, mink, muskrat, opossum, lynx, wolf, and fox. Remains of all these animals have been found near the site of Ft. St. Joseph and are now in the collection of the Indiana Hist. Soc.—G. H. Baker, Sec. of the Society. See also *Mich. Hist. Colls.*, I, 403; VI, 475; XIV, 422.

of France, England, and the United States, it will be necessary to consider the history of her fur trade under each one of these governments. Though the method of trade and the men engaged in it are in many cases the same under two successive régimes, yet it will be seen that each government pursued its own peculiar policy in controlling the trade, and that each régime had its own striking characteristics which distinguished it from the others. Michigan fur trade under the French régime will first be considered.

From its inception, the French policy of trade was monopolistic in character. The exclusive privilege of trading was granted to colonizing companies,[8] which

---

8.   In 1603 some merchants around Rouen, France, formed a colonizing company. They were to put forth every effort to secure large profits in trade.—Brymner, *Canadian Archives*, 1885, xxix; Sheldon, *Hist of Mich.*, 21; *Jes. Rel.*, I, 305; *Ibid*, III, 41-45.
Cardinal Richelieu revoked their privileges in 1627, and the Company of a Hundred Associates was formed, to whom was granted jurisdiction over territory "from Florida to the Arctic Circle"—*Jes. Rel.*, IV, 257.
The Company of a Hundred Associates had a monopoly of the fur trade for fifteen years. In 1644 delegates from the *habitants* of Canada went to France to secure a restriction on this monopoly. In 1645 they secured the right of trade on the condition that they support their government, the garrison, and the religious establishments, paying the government 1000 lbs. of beaver skins, annually, as a Seignioral rent.—*Jes. Rel.*, VIII, 308 (n. 57); XXVII, 77, 137.
"In 1664 was formed the Compagnie des Indes Occidentales; but upon protest of the merchants, the company gave up its monopoly in exchange for the right to levy a duty of one-fourth of the beaver skins and one-tenth of the moose skins imported from Canada. In 1674 this company dissolved, but the king retained the duties in the same form and farmed them out for 350,000 livres. These farmers formed a company sometimes called the Company of the Domain"—La Hontan, *N. V. to N. A.*, I, 91 n; *Jes. Rel.*, L, 147, 247.

attempted to control it by strictly forbidding all trade outside of Montreal. No one was to go searching for furs among the savages, but the latter were to bring them in to this great depot of exchange.[9] Such a scheme was not long successful, because competitors entered the field. Already in 1670 the hardy Briton established a post on the Hudson Bay and began to dispute with the French this lucrative forest commerce,[10] while a class of adventurous Frenchmen, the coureurs de bois, rovers of the forest as they were called, struck boldly into the wilderness, trading with and cheating the savage to their hearts' content, in spite of trading companies and French decrees.[11]

8. *Con.* This was followed by the Company of the Colony in 1700. Margry, *Déc. et étab.*, V, 172-3, 360-1; *Jes. Rel.*, LXV, 273.

9. Brymner, *Canadian Archives*, 1899 (Sup.), 95; Willson, *The Great Company*, I, 17.
Great annual fairs were established at Montreal by order of the king, at which time the Indians came and camped outside the city. Here they met the merchants and bartered their furs for merchandise. There was a similar fair at Three Rivers.—Parkman, *Old Régime*, 303-4.

10. Willson, *The Great Company*, I, 5, 17, 49.

11. Masson, *Les Bourgeois*, I, 4; Brymner, *Canadian Archives*, 1899 (Sup.), 317; Irving, *Astoria*, 20; Parkman, *Old Régime*, 310-15; *N. Y. Col. Docs.*, IX, 140-5, 152-4, 159-60.
M. Du Chesneau in 1679 says, "I have done all in my power. ... I have enacted ordinances against the coureurs de bois; against the merchants who furnished them goods; against the gentlemen and others who harbor them, and even against those who have any knowledge of them and will not inform the justices nearest the spot. All that has been in vain."—*N. Y. Col. Docs.*, IX, 131.
As early as 1673 decrees against the coureurs de bois are noted. Brymner, *Canadian Archives*, 1885, xxxv.
Sulte holds that this class did not arise until about 1670.—*Wis. Hist. Colls.*, X, 41 (n. 2).
"By 1660 they had come to form a distinct class known as coureurs de bois."—Wis. Hist. Soc. *Proceedings*, 1889, 66.

Hence a more aggressive policy was necessary to keep control of the trade and check these lawless adventurers. Thus arose the license system, and decrees were passed forbidding trade among the Indians except by those having a license. Twenty-five of these were to be granted, and each person receiving one was to send out two canoes with three persons in each canoe.[12] To be sure, this policy was modified and changed as time and circumstances demanded, but generally speaking, throughout the entire French régime, trade was restricted. It was under such a system that the early traders of Michigan lived and wrought. But in this spot of the wilderness, far from the reach of justice, men were a law unto themselves, and paddled their canoe according to their own fancy. To show who some of these pioneer traders were, the character of their temporary rendezvous, the fortunes of their more permanent posts and the problems they met and solved or left unsolved, is the aim of this chapter.

Before illegal trade had made the license system necessary, Michigan territory had been invaded by the French and a new field for fur trade opened. In June 1634 Samuel Champlain,[13] the great fur trader, sent Jean Nicolet[14] on a tour of discovery westward,

12. Parkman, *Old Régime*, 305, refers to "Ordres du Roy au sujet de la traité du Canada, 1681." For licenses of trade and amnesty see *N. Y. Col. Docs.*, IX, 152-5, 159, 160, 211, 214, 408, 662, 954, 958; *Jes. Rel.*, LXV, 272; Brymner, *Canadian Archives*, 1899 (Sup.), 77; *Ibid*, 1881-4, 151.
13. For Champlain's relation to early trading companies see *Jes. Rel.*, IV, 256-257.
14. Jean Nicolet came to Quebec in 1618, and in 1620 was sent by Champlain to live among the Algonquins that he might learn their language. He spent nine years among the Nipissings, having his own cabin and household, and fishing and trading for himself. He was recalled by

to find if possible the route to China and make
acquaintance with the Indians beyond Lake Huron
that French trade for peltries might be extended into
that region, or according to Margry, to make peace
with the Winnebagoes in the interest of the fur trade.[15]
With seven Hurons as an escort he took the upper
route from Montreal, crossed to Sault Ste. Marie,
later to the Straits of Mackinac, and thence by Lake
Michigan on to Wisconsin.[16] Sulte holds that he
was not a coureur de bois but an Indian interpreter.[17]
Be that as it may, he had been a trader for several
years[18] and was sent by a man intensely interested in
trade. To be sure he was on a mission designated
as one of discovery, but there can be no question
about that same mission's being partly in the interest
of the fur trade, the all important occupation of
Canada at the time.[19] However, his significance here

14. *Con.* Champlain. Butterfield says that Champlain had been
informed of a tribe living on the borders of the sea,
known as "Men of the Sea," who traded with beardless
men who came to them in canoes. Thinking that these
beardless traders were Japanese or Chinese, he desired to
send some one to them, hoping that thus he might discover
the route to China. So he chose Nicolet because of his
knowledge of Indian life and language.
The tribes mentioned according to Butterfield, were none
other than the Dacotahs who came to trade with the
Winnebagoes. Butterfield, *Early Dis. of N. W.*, 33-43;
Jes. Rel., VIII, 247, 257, 267, 295; *Ibid*, XXIII, 276-7.
15. Margry, *Déc. et étab.*, I, 50.
16. For Nicolet and his career, see Butterfield, *Dis. of N. W.;*
Wis. Hist. Colls., XI, 1-25; VIII, 188-194; index, *Jes. Rel.*
17. Sulte says this class did not arise until 1667, or even 1670.
Wis. Hist. Colls., X, 41.
18. See foot notes 14 and 16.
19. Sulte says, "Agriculture no longer counted; Canada existed
only for the fur trade." *Le Commerce de France*, in Royal
Soc. of Canada *Proceedings*, 2nd. ser., XII, sec. 1, 46-7.
The difficulty experienced in getting men to engage in

lies not so much in that he was a trader landing on Michigan soil, nor that he might have traded while there, but rather in this, that he broke the way for others to follow.

But was he the first trader in this section, or had others preceded him? It is claimed that Champlain visited Saginaw before 1611,[20] that traders were at Sault Ste. Marie as early as 1616,[21] and that coureurs de bois had made the present site of Detroit a stopping place since 1620.[22] Butterfield claims that the first contention is false, that Champlain in 1632 knew nothing whatever of the Saginaw section.[23] Even if he did, it is of no vital concern here, for it did not affect the Michigan fur trade. As to those sojourns at the Sault and the Detroit, probably very few if any peltry seekers reached this section as early as designated. Pluck was far from wanting in the early trader. His was a dare-devil courage that welcomed adventure in the unknown wilderness. Yet lawless, hardened vagabond that he was, he had a body to protect from hunger and cold and a scalp to save from the tomahawk, so that a journey alone, in those primeval days of the Northwest, seems next to an impossibility, because of the difficulties of travel and of securing food, and the hostility of the Indians.

19. *Con.* agriculture in preference to the fur trade shows to what extent it absorbed the interest of everyone at this time. *N. Y. Col. Docs.*, IX, 152-160; Parkman, *Old Régime*, 303.
20. *N. Y. Col. Docs.*, IX, 378.
21. La Hontan, *N. V. to N. A.*, I, 149 n.
22. Schoolcraft, *Nar. Journal of Travels* (ed. 1821), 52. This statement is omitted in later editions.
23. Butterfield, *Early Dis. of N. W.*, 52.—Butterfield's contention is doubtless correct. He seems to have made a careful, painstaking study of the life of Nicolet and, as he calls it, the Discovery of the North West.

Numerous stories are related by the Jesuits of the straits to which the early dwellers among the savages were reduced and of the sufferings endured by them.[24] Le Jeune tells how at one time, being sorely pressed with hunger, he ate the patches of eel skin on his gown, and the good father declared that had it been made of the same stuff, he would have brought it home much shorter. He ate old moose skin much tougher than that of the eel, and went about through the woods biting the ends of branches and gnawing the more tender barks.[25] This reveals but one instance among many, of the sufferings of these men who were on friendly terms with the Indians and partly under their protection and care. What must wandering alone in such wilds have meant?

Then, too, the Indians at first refused to take the missionaries with them. It is doubtful if they were less adverse to the trader. "Being present, on a certain day, at a meeting where the savages discussed sending their young men with merchandise to these more distant tribes," says a Jesuit, "I offered to accompany them, that I might speak of God to those poor people; this somewhat troubled them, for they are unwilling that Frenchmen should have a knowledge of their trade and what they give to other savages for their furs, and this they keep so secret that no one is able to discover it. They described to me the horrible and frightful roads, as they are, indeed; but they magnified the horror of them so as to astound me and divert me from my plan."[26] Such was the attitude

24. *Jes. Rel.*, VIII, 77; *Ibid*, V, 171.
25. *Ibid*, VII, 49.
26. *Ibid*, XXI, 99; see also *Ibid*, VIII, 71, and XXXV, 279.

of some of the tribes even as late as 1640, so that a journey very far westward, particularly into regions entirely unknown, was by no means easily accomplished and must have demanded almost superhuman courage and endurance.

However, when the way had once been traveled and the path broken, so that men knew what lay beyond the Great Fish Lake (Huron), such a journey became less of a problem, and a promise of rich returns in peltries was a magnetic force luring many a coureur de bois to follow the path into the western wilds pointed out by Nicolet and his men in 1634. Some came to stay with the Indians in the haunts of the beaver, two, three, and even four years; others went merely as far as the Sault, or Michilimackinac, to meet the red men and other coureurs de bois, to obtain from them peltries in exchange for merchandise and brandy.[27] These were the lawless traders, the unlicensed dealers who built no permanent posts, but under certain leaders like Daniel Greyselon Du Lhut erected rude forts or palisades at various points which they occupied as long as it suited their purpose, and then abandoned them for the next comer.[28] Just what was the exact character of these temporary abodes, it is difficult to say. They challenge our interest but practically nothing is known of them beyond the fact that they existed. No doubt they were rude huts or tents, on or near some great Indian camping ground

27. *N. Y. Col. Docs.*, IX, 153-4. Turner says, "Wisconsin was a favorite resort of these adventurers. By the time of the arrival of the Jesuits the *coureurs de bois* had made themselves entirely at home upon our lakes." Wis. Hist. Soc. *Proceedings*, 1889, 66.
28. Parkman, *Old Régime*, 313.

where prospects for trade were most promising, or by some streams where fish were abundant. These men, who easily stand in the front rank of the pioneer traders of Michigan, were not learned fellows. They left no records of their wanderings, hence many facts concerning their life necessarily must be mere conjecture.

Médard Chouart, Sieur de Groseilliers, Pièrre Radisson, and Robert de la Salle deserve to be ranked among the forerunners of Michigan traders. The first two are said to have spent the entire winter of 1659-60 at Sault Ste. Marie. Ardent devotees of the peltry trade, no doubt anxious to find new fields for harvest, they had decided to explore the region of the Great Lakes. In the middle of June, 1658, with twenty-nine Frenchmen and six Indians they left Three Rivers and passed through the Straits of Mackinac to Wisconsin, where they spent the winter. In October, 1659, they returned to Michigan, and it was that winter which they spent with the Indians at the Sault, returning to Green Bay, Wisconsin, in the spring of 1660. The same year they departed for Quebec with sixty canoes filled with peltries.[29]

La Salle, with Father Louis Hennepin, Henry de Tonty, and twenty-five others, following the lower route, came to Detroit, and from there pushed on to Green Bay, Wisconsin. After loading his boat, the *Griffin*, with furs, he sent her back, while he and a few others struck boldly across to the Michigan shore and went down to the mouth of the St. Joseph River.

---

29. Margry, *Déc. et étab.*, I, 53-55; *Wis. Hist. Colls.*, X, 292-8; XI, 64-96; Winsor, *Nar. and Crit. Hist.*, IV, 168-73; *Minn. Hist. Colls.*, V, 401, 402; *Ibid*, VII, 47-59.

There he established a fort, and, leaving a few men in charge, went into Illinois and beyond. Desiring to return, he waited in vain for the *Griffin* to come and carry him home. There was but one conclusion; this little craft with men and fur must be lost, and La Salle must needs find other means of returning. Nothing daunted, he gathered his courage and trudged across the Lower Peninsula, reaching the Detroit in April, 1680; the first cross-country tramp made in Michigan.[30]

Surely the Jesuit, that black-robed priest of frontier life, who followed hard and fast in the foot steps of the trader, must be accorded a place among these early scouts of civilization. Wherever the fur trader went he followed, for both were interested in the savage, —one seeking him for his peltries, the other for the salvation of his soul. Though not a trader, yet, at times, this follower of the Cross did trade. He had his influence and certainly his say in this early commerce, and it is in his records that knowledge of pioneer trade must be sought. That realistic word-picture of the trading post Mackinac, with its lawlessness and vice, its drunken brawls and illicit trade, so vividly portrayed by Father Carheil, is, no doubt, typical of the trader's life in the majority of frontier posts.[31]

These men were not averse to trade, but helped to make it possible and profitable. By their kindness to the Indian they made him well disposed toward the French, and thus opened the way to many western tribes for their trade.[32] Mackenzie says of them,

30.   *Mich. Hist. Colls.*, XIV, 657.
31.   *Jes. Rel.*, LXV, 189-253.
32.   *Ibid*, XXXVI, 237.

if these missionaries did not obtain their object, they were yet of great service to the commanders who engaged in those distant expeditions, and they spread the fur trade.[33] They realized its value to their native country. Father Carheil says, "I desire the good of both religion and the Trade, which you are obliged to keep in accord one with the other, without Ever separating one from the other."[34]

The rule of the seventh general congregation of the Society forbade all kinds of commerce and business, under any pretext whatever, but this was not wholly satisfactory to the fathers. Le Jeune tells how some of them sent him word that they were forbidden "to even look at, from the corner of our eyes, or touch with the ends of our fingers, the skins of any of the animals." They questioned this; for, said they, peltry is not only the best thing and easiest to make use of in this country but also a coin of greatest value. If occasionally one of them got into their hands they did not scruple to use it in any way of purchase. They also sent some old elk to their fathers among the Hurons.[35] Crépieul held that fishing and hunting the hares and martens was proper when necessary and for recreation, provided the missionary did not get too fond of them.[36] Father Vimont obtained Dès Châstelet's consent that the prohibition of trade with

---

33. Mackenzie, *Voyages*, I, v. They were of mutual helpfulness; Turner says, "The Jesuits followed in the trader's steps, and received his protection and their first missions were on the sites of his trading posts." Wis. Hist. Society *Proceedings*, 1889, 67; see also Winsor, *Nar. and Crit. Hist.*, IV, 184.
34. *Jes. Rel.*, LXV, 245.
35. *Ibid*, IX, 171-5.
36. *Ibid*, LXIII, 265.

the Indians should not apply to the Jesuits, if they carried it on quietly.[37] That they were not hostile to the fur trade and the fur trader as such, is certain. If they are found railing against the traders at Mackinac and later against men like Cadillac, it is not because they opposed fostering the trade, but because of the methods of trade pursued, methods that seemed to neutralize all their efforts for good.

Men like Nicolet, Groseilliers, Radisson and La Salle helped to open the way and make entrance easier for other traders, but these men were mere sojourners, who came, went, and were forgotten. The coureurs de bois were rovers, as their name implies. To be sure, throughout the State they had their places to which they annually repaired to meet and barter with the savage, but usually theirs was a wandering life and they did not hesitate to abandon their temporary rendezvous, when a more lucrative spot was discovered. The Jesuit was not quite such a migrant. True, he also sought the Indian on his hunting ground, and, occasionally, tarried with the coureur de bois at his temporary fort; but his mission was, as a rule, found

---

37.   *Ibid*, XXVII, 99.   Father Brébeuf did not favor trade by the Jesuit.   In one place he says, "At last it is understood, from our actions and our truths [of religion] that we have not come either to buy skins or carry on any traffic but solely to teach them and win them to Christ." *Jes. Rel.*, XI, 15.

In 1646, 260 lbs. of beaver skins were taken from one Ursuline priest.   *Jes. Rel.*, XXX, 183.

Parkman in speaking of the missionaries and trade says, "This charge of trading .... is vehemently reiterated in many quarters, including the official dispatches of the Governor of Canada, while so far as I can discover the Jesuits never distinctly denied it."—*Dis. of the Great West*, 36.

where permanent posts had been established. And
it is these permanent trading centers, the marts of
exchange for voyageur, coureur de bois, and Indian,
the centers of the mission, the homes of the soldiers
and commandant, the places of the annual feasts and
revels of all traders, that next claim our attention.
There were but few of these in Michigan during the
French régime, namely, at Sault Ste. Marie, Mackinac,
Detroit, and St. Joseph.

Sault Ste. Marie was first to assume importance as
a trading center.[38]   It was the rallying point for most
of the savages in this section,[39] for this was the great
fish region, much sought by the Indians.[40]   Naturally,
it became early the center of a wide-spreading fur
trade, a position it held until Mackinaw rose into
prominence.[41]   Mention has already been made of the
claim that traders came to this spot as early as 1616.
Another visit is reported as taking place in 1641,
when, it is said, the Frenchmen met the Potawatomis
fleeing from their enemies.[42]   Hither came Charles
Raymbault and Isaac Jogues in 1641, and held the
first mission in Michigan, a temporary mission, how-

38. La Hontan, N. V. to N. W., I, 149.
39. The chief of these were the ones called by the French,
     Saulteurs; in 1669-71 about 150 in number. These
     united with them three other nations, of more than 550
     persons. Besides these four nations, there were seven
     others dependent on the mission at the Sault. Two
     nations, entirely nomadic, came there to fish in the
     summer and went north to hunt in the winter. Six other
     nations wandered hither from time to time to fish. *Jes.
     Rel.*, LIV, 133.
40. *Jes. Rel.*, LIV, 129, 131; *Ibid*, L, 263; LV, 157; Sheldon,
     Hist. of Mich., 25.
41. *Ibid*, I, 317.
42. La Hontan, N. V. to N. A., I, 149; N. Y. Col. Docs., IX,
     153.

ever, which was permanently established by Father
Marquette in 1669. A party of Jesuits arriving in
March of that year, are reported as having found there
twenty-five French traders who claimed that a most
profitable commerce had sprung up.[43] Here in the
presence of several Frenchmen and fourteen Indian
nations, Monsieur de Saint Lusson in May, 1671,
took possession of this region in the name of the
French.[44] But by 1689, Sault Ste. Marie was practically abandoned as a trading post and from then on
formed merely a station on the trade route to the
Northwest, and was not re-established until De
Repentigny was sent there in 1750 to re-occupy the
post.[45]

Of all Michigan trading posts, there was none that
grew to greater importance in the fur régime than
Michilimackinac, and that importance was assumed
early. Nicolet passed through the Straits in 1634,[46]
and Denonville claims that French traders lived there
in 1648.[47] That contention is doubtless true, for
located on the highway usually traversed in those days
to Wisconsin and the wilderness beyond, it must
early have become a resting place and a depot of
exchange for traders on their pilgrimages to more
distant regions. Parkman calls it the chief resort of
the coureurs de bois, whence in groups of two or three
they started out to roam hundreds of miles in the
savage wilderness.[48] This mart was a splendid place

---

43. Willson, *The Great Company*, I, 51.
44. *Jes. Rel.*, LV, 107-9 and 113; *N. Y. Col. Docs.*, IX, 383.
45. La Hontan, *N. V. to N. A.*, I, 149; Wis. Hist. Soc. *Proceed-
    ings*, 1889, 73.
46. Said to be the first white man to pass through these Straits.
47. *N. Y. Col. Docs.*, IX, 383.
48. Parkman, *Old Régime*, 313.

for the Jesuit to corner the red man when he came to trade, and point out to him the straight and narrow path, so he founded his mission here;[49] and France realizing its key position, sent hither soldiers and commandants, that trade might be better protected.[50]

That there was urgent need of such protection was soon realized. A peaceful pursuit and usurpation of the fur trade by any one people could scarcely be thought of. From the beginning of the fur trade régime to its close a bitter warfare was waged for the possession of this "golden fleece" of the New World; monopolizing companies competed with coureurs de bois, Indian tribe with Indian tribe, French with English, English with American, independent traders with trading companies, and vice versa. It was a competition that lasted until the forest was stripped of its rich supply of peltries.

The French authorities could do nothing with its coureurs de bois, for they roamed where they pleased through Michigan forests, as elsewhere; but a more dangerous enemy had soon to be reckoned with. By 1670 the English had established a powerful trading rival on Hudson Bay, which lured Indians and coureurs de bois from the upper posts, because they paid higher for peltries and offered cheaper goods.[51] Father Nouvel writes to the Governor of New France from Sault Ste. Marie in 1673: "We try as much as we can.... to incline them [the Indians] to continue their intercourse with the French. But already we see that the establishment of the English on the Great Bay of

49. Jes. Rel., I, 34-35; Wis. Hist. Colls., XIV, 5-6.
50. Jes. Rel., LXII, 274; LXV, 189 ff.
51. Ibid, LXVII, 125; Ibid, LXVI, 173; Winsor, Nar. and Crit. Hist., V, 3.

the North, and the proximity of the Iroquois, with whom the Missisakis have pursued their winter hunting, will cause a decided prejudice against the colony. The English have already diverted a great many of the inland savages who visit Lake Superior, and attracted them to themselves by their great liberality; and the Iroquois have sent considerable presents to all these nations, to confirm, they say, the peace that Onnontio made,—but rather to get their peltries, with which the Iroquois are expecting these tribes to respond to their presents."[52] That tribe, willing allies of the Briton, declared war on the Ottawas and the Hurons who were dwelling around Michilimackinac, hoping by this means to get possession of their commerce.[53]

The British and the Flemings of New York also had their eyes on Michilimackinac trade, scheming to secure at least a part if not all of it. In 1686 a small party of these arrived, traded with the savages and were invited by them to come again. This invitation was accepted and soon a second expedition was planned. Two bands, one led by Rooseboom and the other by McGregor, each floating an English flag and armed with an English passport, set out for this upper post. Rooseboom came on ahead. With him were some savages of the nation Lupes and some Iroquois who were to serve as guides and hunt for food. By the influence of the latter they obtained the services of an influential Indian through whom they hoped to

52. *Jes. Rel.*, LVII, 21.
53. *Ibid*, LXIII, 281-83; Parkman, *Frontenac and New France*, 145-7; *N. Y. Col. Docs.*, IX, 866; Brymner, *Canadian Archives*, 1899 (Sup.), 282.

facilitate their reception among the tribes they intended to visit. An abundance of cheap merchandise and quantities of rum were brought as a bait to entice the Indians and the forest rovers from their loyalty to the French; but they reckoned without their host. Licensed and unlicensed traders joined forces against the enemy, prompted perhaps less by patriotic zeal than by fear of their bread and butter. La Durantaye with as curious, ill-assorted a little army, no doubt, as ever gave chase to an Englishman, set out to meet them, and he soon settled the matter with Rooseboom by capturing him and his goods, distributing the latter among his Indian allies. Then he proceeded to Detroit where he was joined by Du Lhut and Tonty with their army of coureurs de bois and Indians, and together they started towards Niagara. They encountered the second band on the way and these, too, were captured.[54]

So this attempt to rob France of Michilimackinac trade ended in failure. As a military encounter it was perhaps of little significance, but it wrought mischief among the Hurons and Ottawas and made them restless under French rule. They saw here a chance to buy cheaper goods and get more for their peltries. They realized it was an opportunity to make peace with the Iroquois on their own account, the very thing the French did not want, for they preferred keeping these tribes dependent in order to keep their trade which might otherwise go to the English.[55] The sentiments expressed by Beschefer show to some extent the importance that Frenchmen

54. *Jes. Rel.*, LXIII, 281-83; Parkman, *Frontenac and New France*, 145-7; *N. Y. Col. Docs.*, IX, 866; Brymner, *Canadian Archives*, 1899 (Sup.), 282.
55. *Jes. Rel.*, LXIV, 11-12; *Wis. Hist. Colls.*, XVI, 162.

attached to the expedition: "Had these parties not been taken," says he, "the entire trade of Canada would have been ruined, because nearly all the furs come from the Ottawa, and had they been free to go themselves to trade in New York they would certainly have sided with the Iroquois against us."[56]

English effort to snatch from the French the upper commerce was a powerful inducement for the latter to establish a post in the environs of the Detroit River, and so shut the door to this region against these aggressive Britons and their capable Iroquois allies. The first expedition of the English had been made in the early months of 1686.[57] In June of that same year Denonville ordered Du Lhut who was then commandant at Michilimackinac, to establish a combined fort and trading post at the Detroit with a garrison of fifty men, choosing an advantageous position, that he might control the strait and protect the savages hunting there, giving them a place of refuge against their enemies. Du Lhut at once repaired thither with fifty coureurs de bois and built a stockade on the strait.[58]

On June seventh, the following year, La Durantaye took formal possession of the region for France, "in the presence of the reverend Father Angeleran, superior of the mission of the Outaouas at Michilimackinac, of Ste. Marie de Sault, of the Miamis, of the Illinois, of the Baie des Puans, and of the Sioux, of M. de la

56. *Jesuit Relations*, LXIII, 283.
57. The letter of Denonville to the French minister was written in May. Margry, *Déc. et étab.*, V, 14.
58. Margry, *Déc. et étab.*, V, 22, 23; *Mich. Hist. Colls.* XIV, 659; *Jes. Rel.*, LXII, 274; *Wis. Hist. Colls.*, XVI, 125-7.

Forest late commandant at the fort at St. Louis at the Illinois...and of M. de Beauvais, our lieutenant of the Fort St. Joseph at the strait of Lake Huron and Erie."[59] The garrison of coureurs de bois, longing for their old free life, and wishing to turn traders again, cheerfully placed the fort in the hands of Louis-Armand La Hontan, who came there as commandant in September, 1687. This was a short-lived fort. France was waging war with the Iroquois, and La Hontan, hearing that Fort Niagara had been deserted and, as he says, that Denonville "had a mind to clap up a Peace," concluded that this post would be of no use; so he set fire to the fort and sailed with his crew to Michilimackinac.[60] Thus ended Fort St. Joseph on the Detroit.

A strong effort was made in 1686 to get the trade in Michigan and all this western region under better control. Denonville issued a proclamation in that year, addressed to the commandants at the various posts, the traders, and the Indians. Besides asking them to be in readiness to go against the Iroquois, he commanded all the western traders to deliver their furs either to Durantaye and Enjalran, at Michilimackinac, or to Du Lhut at Detroit. They were to be under the command of Durantaye and must furnish a certificate of their trade from Enjalran. The merchants, too, must give a statement of the goods they furnished to the traders.[61]

When the intercolonial wars began in 1689, Michigan trade suffered, as did trade elsewhere, for peace was

59.   Can. Roy. Soc., *Proceedings*, 1894, Sec. I, 79 n.
60.   La Hontan, *N. V. to N. A.*, I, 161-3.
61.   Brymner, *Canadian Archives*, 1899 (Sup.), 84.

as necessary to this branch of commerce as to any other. Intercourse with Montreal and Quebec was cut off; hostile Iroquois urged on by the English, were making incursions into French territory and falling upon French traders who attempted to carry furs to market, while the English, ever prone to cause their old enemy the French every harm possible, constantly held out a bait to lure all Indians to their side; a thing which would have been fatal to trade, to say nothing of its effect on their military fortunes in the new world. Many French posts were abandoned; but Michilimackinac, Michigan's only post during the early years of the war, held her own. It is said that M. Perrot who was then its commandant, though a man of great ability, had his powers tried to the utmost. Not only had he to meet and solve problems of war confronting him, but he must needs harmonize and subjugate the many adverse and discordant elements gathered there, in the shape of soldiers and priests, licensed trader, coureurs de bois, and Indian allies deprived of their former occupation; assuredly, no mean task.[62]

When, in 1694, La Motte Cadillac took charge of the post, there were present about two hundred French troops, besides the coureurs de bois, traders and artisans, while at certain seasons thousands of Indians assembled.[63]

After the abandonment of La Salle's fort at the mouth of the St. Joseph, the history of this river valley, as far as known, remains a silent chapter until the opening of the eighteenth century. It is readily

62.   Sheldon, *Hist. of Mich.*, 68-9.
63.   Ross and Catlin, *Landmarks of Detroit*, 33.

seen that, affording as it did an opportunity for penetrating further into the State, it early became a
favorite route for voyageurs from Michilimackinac.
Charlevoix tells us that it was a river much frequented
by Indians,[64] and where the Indians congregated, the
French traders were sure to come. Here dwelt the
Miamis, where formerly the Potawatomi held sway.
With the Kankakee, this river later became an important trading route into the Illinois country.[65]

To form an estimate of the amount and value of furs
in Michigan during the seventeenth century seems an
impossibility, for peltries from posts like Sault Ste.
Marie and Michilimackinac are not representative of
furs gathered in Michigan alone, but came from other
regions, such as Wisconsin, Illinois, and beyond.
Pioneer traders kept no accounts of what they gathered
in their particular sections. Little care had they for
aught else except the beaver pelt. Then, too, Michigan
was but a spot in a great western wilderness, a small
part of a great Canadian province of which the fur
trade was the chief source of wealth. So estimates
were made for the province as a whole and not for
some small section of it. For example, Mackenzie
says the produce of the year 1798 was 181,150 furred
animals of which 106,000 were beavers.[66]

To quote prices of furs of this century is of little
significance, because in those good old trading days
the French soon discovered that the Indian knew little
of the value of fur and readily exchanged the costliest
peltries for whatever tickled his fancy, even though
it were a mere trifle. Out in the woods each trader

---

64. Charlevoix, *Journal of V. to N. A.*, II, 94.
65. *Wis. Hist. Colls.*, XVI, 372.
66. Mackenzie, *Voyages*, I, xxiv.

often set his own price. A good drink could buy almost anything the red man had, for he was always thirsty. So while trade was in its infancy, an enormous profit accrued to the successful trader, at times a profit of from six to seven hundred per cent.[67]

67. La Hontan, *N. V. to N. A.*, I, 100, 101.
As to the value of beaver, Sulte gives the following table for 1665; he says, at that time the savage exchanged a beaver with the French for any of the following articles: one small cloak, two pounds of powder, four pounds of lead, two swords, two hatchets, eight table knives, ten folding knives, and twenty-five awls; two beavers, for a medium-sized cloak, three for a large-sized one, or one Iroquois blanket; four, for a woolen blanket, six for a white Normandy blanket, or one gun. He also compares the prices of the English with those of the French:

	Montreal			Albany
1 jug brandy for 1 beaver..................				6 jugs
8 pounds powder for 4 beaver..............				1 beaver
1 gun	" 5 "	....	2	"
40 lb. lead	" 3 "	....	1	"
1 red blanket	" 2 "	....	1	"
1 white blanket	" 2 "	....	1	"
1 large coat	" 2 "	....	1	"
4 shirts	" 2 "	....	1	"
10 pair hose	" 2 "	....	1	"

Sulte, *Le Commerce de France*, in Royal Soc. of Canada *Proceedings*, Second ser., XII, Pt. 1, sec. 1, 45-6.
La Hontan quotes the following prices:

Winter beavers, alias Muscovy per lb.	4 livres	..10 sous
Fat beavers per lb................	5 "	..0 "
Beavers taken in autumn per lb.....	3 "	..0 "
Dry or common beaver per lb.......	3 "	..0 "
Summer beaver per lb.............	3 "	..0 "
Skins of silver colored foxes apiece...	4 "	..0 "
Martens apiece...................	1 "	..0 "
Prettiest sort of Martens apiece.....	4 "	..0 "
Red and smooth otters apiece......	2 "	..0 "
Winter and brown otters apiece.....	4 "	..10 "
Finest black bears apiece.........	7 "	..0 "
Muskrats apiece.................	0 "	..6 "
Wolves apiece...................	2 "	..10 "

—La Hontan, *N. V. to N. A.*, I, 379-80.

Sale of liquor to the savages by traders must be reckoned with in any study of the fur trade, for it had its influence in every trading section. The Indian imbibed a taste and love for the white man's brandy, so strong that he would gladly exchange the costliest furs for a drink. Drunken brawls, lawlessness and fraud were the natural outcome, and while the missionary never ceased to rail against the evil, the trader taxed his brain to find some means of evading decrees passed against it.[68] How to destroy, or at least control it, remained an unsolved problem throughout the entire fur régime.[69] The French claimed that to prohibit entirely the sale of liquor to the Indian meant ruin to trade, as long as coureurs de bois and Englishmen furnished it in abundance; for the savage carried his peltries to where he found his fire water.[70]

Nevertheless, the French Government attempted to put a stop to the traffic. Champlain, in 1633, ordered that the sale of liquor be prohibited except under strong control.[71] By 1660 it had gained such excess that Bishop Laval[72] forbade the traffic on penalty

68. See Fr. Carheil's account of the evils of liquor among traders at Michilimackinac, in *Jes. Rel.*, LXV, 195, 199.
69. For the attempts to check the liquor traffic in connection with trade, see p. 26.
70. *N. Y. Col. Docs.*, IX, 777; *Wis. Hist. Colls.*, XVI, 230, 336.
71. La Hontan, *N. V. to N. W.*, I, 94 n.
72. Bishop Laval says of the savages and brandy: "Drink is a demon that robs them of their reason, and so inflames their passion that, after returning from the chase richly laden with beaver skins, instead of furnishing their families with provisions, clothing, and other necessary supplies, they drink away the entire proceeds in one day and are forced to pass the winter in nakedness, famine, and all sorts of deprivations. There have been some whose mania was so extraordinary that, after stripping themselves of everything for liquor, they sold even their own

of excommunication.[73] Frontenac tried to compromise the matter during his first governorship, by prohibiting the carrying of liquor to the woods and allowing a moderate sale in the colony.[74]

The evils of this trade being brought to the attention of Louis XIV, he issued a decree against it in 1679. This provided a punishment for those who took brandy, or had it taken, to the savages; a fine of one hundred livres for the first offense, three hundred for the second, and corporal punishment for the third.[75]

But the trader, that resourceful vagabond of the woods, was clever enough to evade this decree. What he could not sell, he could give away; which is just what he did, according to Mackenzie.[76] In 1694 the king forbade the transportation of brandy to Michigan for trading purposes;[77] but royal decrees and threats from afar meant little in this rude frontier, so governor and commandants winked at its importation and sale, while the blame was heaped on the shoulders of the coureurs de bois.[78]

---

72. *Con.* children to obtain the means of intoxication. Children, too, when they were overcome with drink beat their parents without being punished for it," [etc.]. *Jes. Rel.,* XLVI, 103.
73. *Jes. Rel.,* XLVI, 105. This was soon revoked. The death penalty was added later.
74. La Hontan, *N. V. to N. A.,* I, 94.
75. Cadillac Papers, *Mich. Hist. Colls.,* XXXIII, 704.
76. Mackenzie, *Voyages,* I, vi.
77. Cadillac's letter of August 3, 1695, pub. in Sheldon, *Hist. of Mich.,* 73.
78. Cadillac Papers, *Mich. Hist. Colls.,* XXXIII, 704; *N. Y. Col., Docs.,* IX, 777; Margry, *Déc. et étab.,* V, 12.
    Even the king approved giving it in small doses, advising that the savages be made to understand that the French were giving it more from a desire to please than through inclination. *Wis. Hist. Colls.,* XVII, 158.

As the liquor law was practically a dead letter, so also was the decree which bade that only licensed traders could trade; and accordingly illicit forest commerce prevailed everywhere. Of course, all trade by the coureurs de bois must needs be so designated; but these rangers were not the only lawless traders, according to Carheil. In speaking of the soldiers' life at Michilimackinac, he said that their only occupation as well as that of the commandant was trade with the savages, a trade which legally belonged to regularly licensed voyageurs. In spite of all precautions, a considerable portion of peltries was secured by the former, "through an infinite number of hidden ways and by secret intelligence with the savages." When appeal was made to the commandant, he claimed nothing could be done, as a secret understanding existed between voyageurs and soldiers; this, said Carheil, was a mere excuse; soldiers and commandant were only trying to accommodate each other in carrying on contraband trade.[79] Champigny testifies to the truthfulness of this. He says that there was practically no discipline among the soldiers. They gave up their pay to the captain, that they might leave their quarters and roam at will among the savages to secure peltries.[80]

Such incessant pursuit of trade by each and all, could have but one result; markets were filled to over-

78. *Con.* Cadillac was accused of permitting its sale at Michili-mackinac, also soldiers and garrisons.
    Denonville in a letter to the Minister in 1686 speaks of those (no doubt the coureurs de bois) who against the orders of the king brought one hundred boats of brandy to Michilimackinac. Margry, *Déc. et étab.*, V, 12.
79. *Jes. Rel.*, LXV, 213-15, 245.
80. Letters of Champigny to French Minister, 1698, *Wis. Hist. Colls.*, XVI, 174-5.

flowing with beaver pelts, and prices fell.[81]   France
sought to remedy the evil, and forbade all trade in
the upper country; a command easily given, but not
so readily obeyed, though M. de Champigny put
forth every effort to have it enforced.   He had it
registered with the supreme council and published
throughout the colony with instructions to issue
copies in distant places, wherever the French traded.[82]
It was suggested that such posts as Michilimackinac
be   abandoned.[83]   Voyageurs   were   recalled   and
amnesties offered the coureurs de bois if they would
cease their forest traffic.   But all efforts seemed in
vain.   The forest swarmed with traders, bent on
enriching themselves in this lucrative forest mine.[84]

Carheil says that the very men whom the French
authorities sent to Michilimackinac with the grants
of amnesty came solely to trade, prolonging their time
as much as they could, so as to sell all their wares to
those whom they came to recall and thus furnish the
latter the means to carry on trade.[85]   To attempt to
stop   trade   while   Frenchmen   roamed   at   will   was

81.   Brymner, *Canadian Archives*, 1899 (Sup.), 317.
82.   Cadillac Papers, *Mich. Hist. Colls.*, XXXIII, 72-3.
      The idea was to leave the missionaries among the Indians to
      maintain their allegiance to the French.   Carheil suggests
      a return to the old method of trade, having the savages
      bring their furs directly to Montreal. *Jes. Rel.*, LXV,
      221-5.
83.   *Ibid.*, 73.
84.   *Ibid*, 75.
      Sieur de Tonty had gone to the country of the Assinibouelles
      where there was beaver in abundance.   Sieur de la Seur
      had formed a settlement on the Mississippi, where he
      pretended there were copper and lead mines, but men
      suspected that they were beaver mines instead. *Mich.
      Hist. Colls.*, XXXIII, 74-75.
85.   *Jes. Rel.*, LXV, 215.

futile. In 1698 Champigny wrote to the French
minister: "I repeat to you all I said last year about
the necessity of leaving no Frenchmen, garrison of
troops, or other men at Michilimackinac, among the
Illinois, or the Miamis, or at fort Frontenac, or the
other distant places, if you wish absolutely to put an
end to the beaver trade here."[86]

How to get his pelts to market and secure merchandise for exchange became now a considerable problem for the trader. He dared not do it himself, for to
show that he was trading in spite of decrees against it
would certainly mean imprisonment; so, ingeniously,
he hit upon sending the savage. That dusky ally
was easily trained; he visited the colony and carried
on all necessary transactions, "very cleverly," says
Champigny, "appearing to be acting for himself."[87]

Michilimackinac was a veritable nest of illicit
traders. Governor Callières sent Sieur Alphonse de
Tonty to bring them to Montreal, but only twenty
followed him. The others, eighty-four in number,
had planned a trading trip down the Mississippi to
the establishment there, where, said they, thirty had
already gone with ten canoes loaded with beaver.[88]

That the orders for all French to return or leave
Michilimackinac was not obeyed, is evident from a
letter written by Louis XIV to Messrs. de Callières
and de Champigny, May 31, 1701, in which he says:
"In regard to the eighty-four who had not yet rejoined
last year, and the greater portion of whom had proceeded to the Mississippi, his Majesty has been in-

---

86. Adapted from *Wis. Hist. Colls.*, XVI, 174-5.
87. *Ibid.*
88. Letter of Gov. Callières. *Wis. Hist. Colls.*, XVI, 201.

formed of the reasons which have detained them in the woods, and has been pleased to take it into favorable consideration, being strongly persuaded that the clemency he is pleased to extend them, will engage them to a more prompt obedience in the future."[89] His Royal Highness had a bigger problem on hand to make these western subjects obey, than they had in contriving to evade his commands; for, if too severe, he might drive the coureurs de bois to join hands with his enemy the English.

So the close of the seventeenth century saw Michigan forests filled with illicit traders, while the markets were overstocked with beaver, and French officials were putting forth every effort to lessen the supply. Sault Ste. Marie and Fort St. Joseph on the Detroit had been abandoned, and a strong but unsuccessful effort made to recall all traders from Michilimackinac. This latter post, far from having reached the pinnacle of its trading career, nevertheless had assumed considerable importance. It alone of the early posts had weathered the storm of English and Flemish attack and held its own in Iroquois struggles and intercolonial war. But at the dawn of the eighteenth century a strong rival arose in the Lower Peninsula to dispute with it the monoply of Michigan trade and practically cause its abandonment, by drawing from its environs the savages, so necessary for successful trade. The story of that fur-trading rival will now be told.

89. *N. Y. Col. Docs.*, IX, 721.

CHAPTER II

Detroit the Great Depot of Trade

WHEN at the opening of the eighteenth century the little trade center Detroit was established, it at once assumed the lead in peltry traffic. Sault Ste. Marie had been abandoned, Michilimackinac had dwindled to insignificance, and the St. Joseph trade had been largely absorbed. Detroit was practically Michigan's only depot of trade during the earlier years of its existence, dominating and controlling her entire forest commerce.

Naturally the question arises, for what purpose and by whom was the Detroit post founded? The fur trade, the French desire to control it, to continue it, and to keep it from the grasp of the British was, generally, the impelling motive leading the pioneers to seize key points and establish posts there. The English frontier line was fast moving westward, and at the close of the seventeenth century, British traders were coming dangerously near to territory claimed by France. Rivalry for the fur trade was becoming more intense, and it was necessary to check these advancing Englishmen, so keen for trade.[1] The strategic position of the Detroit was fully appreciated by the French, for already in 1686 they had taken steps to shut out the English, Dutch, and Iroquois from the upper country commerce by ordering Du Lhut

---

1. Weiser's Journal, *Western Travels*, I, 19.

to establish a post there.[2] But this had been abandoned[3] and France had made no effort to re-occupy and to make a permanent post there. The door stood open, by which the enemy could go in and out among the French Indian allies, and get control of the Detroit and the fur trade of the upper countries.

Antoine de la Mothe Cadillac, commandant at Michilimackinac, looking abroad for more fruitful fields of trade, decided that the Detroit was the very place he wanted. To better carry out his project of founding a post there, he went to France to interview Count Pontchartrain and place before him the advantages of such an establishment.[4] To get control of the strait, said he, would serve not only to advance trade, but to preserve it. It was one of the best places to hold the Iroquois and English in check and prevent them from carrying on traffic in furs with the western tribes.[5] It had yet another advantage; a great variety of peltries could be secured in its environs; elks, moose, wolves, bear, beaver, otters, muskrats, and lynxes.[6] The matter was referred to Chev. de Callières and M. de Champigny, and on October 4, 1701, the former notified the king that he had sent Cadillac with more than a hundred soldiers and Canadians to establish a post at the Detroit.[7] Such in brief is the history of its founding.

Its trading career under the French may be divided

2. Margry, *Déc. et étab.*, V, 22 and 23; *Wis. Hist. Colls.*, XVI, 125-7.
3. La Hontan, *N. V. to N. A.*, I, 163.
4. *Mich. Hist. Colls.*, XXIX, 256; *Ibid*, XIV, 662.
5. *Ibid*, I, 350; XIV, 662; XXXIII, 132, 139; 198-9, 168-9.
6. *Ibid*, XXXIII, 135, 144, 200; Farmer, *Hist. of Detroit*, 11.
7. *Mich. Hist. Colls.*, XXXIII, 107.

into three fairly well marked periods. First came the brief and inefficient rule of the Company of the Colony, who, soon weary of an undertaking which proved less lucrative than had been expected, resigned Detroit and its trade into the hands of Cadillac; the latter, having founded the post, doubtless had hoped to control it from the first. His régime, during which the colony was firmly established and trade flourished, was followed by a period in which Detroit passed from the dominance of one master to that of another. The reign of some of these was so brief that little, practically nothing, could be done for the advancement of the post. Others were in control longer but they thought more of filling their own pockets than the coffers of the colony.

This infant frontier post, founded not merely for trade alone, but for military and agricultural purposes as well,[8] had many enemies. The Iroquois were hostile; for, not only did it seem an encroachment upon their hunting grounds, but it shut them from the upper lakes and interrupted their passage to the Mississippi.[9] The governor general was accused of opposing it; because it was not established by his command but by that of the king, and because it interfered with the interests of many persons in colonial service. The Indians of the upper country were in the habit of going annually to Montreal, often bringing with them rich and costly furs to the officers, while return presents were given at the king's expense.

8. *Ibid*, I, 350.
9. *Ibid*, XXXIII, 168-9; VIII, 428.

5

This new colony threatened to put an end to these profitable visits.[10]

Cadillac doubted the sincerity of the Jesuits' professed friendship, suspecting that their outwardly complaisant acquiescence in his plans was not entirely genuine, since he and the Jesuit priests had often clashed,[11] and the latter may have felt that the rise and growth of Detroit was certain to weaken Michilimackinac. They were thought to have formed with Sir de la Forest and Sir de Tonty, a project for establishing a post among the Miamis in order to ruin Detroit trade.[12] Cadillac says: "If our colony were not full of envy, disunion, cabal and intrigue, no opposition would have been offered to taking possession of a post, [which is] so advantageous that, if it were separated from all those we [now] have, we should be compelled in a short time to abandon all; for it is that alone which will make the colony and its commerce entirely safe, and cause the certain ruin of English colonies. For that reason it is very important that

10. *Ibid*, VIII, 430-31, XXXIII, 148. It was said that if too much license was given Detroit it would ruin Montreal merchants. *Ibid*, XXXIII, 156.
11. *Jes. Rel.*, LXV, 272.
     In a letter to Pontchartrain, Cadillac says: "You wished me to be a friend of the Jesuits and have no trouble with them. After much reflection I have found only three ways in which this can be accomplished. That is, to let them do as they please, to do whatever they please, and say nothing whatever they do." (Sheldon, *Hist. of Mich.*, 102.) Cadillac said of Joseph Marest and Etienne Carheil that they were employing all means to prevent savages from coming, as could be seen from the councils held Oct. 30 and Dec. 4, 1701. Margry, *Déc. et étab.*, V, 205-6.
12. Margry, *Déc. et étab.*, V, 240-41.

it should not pass into other hands which would be inevitable if we deferred taking it any longer."[13]

If Cadillac founded the colony, fully intending to be its master and control its trade,[14] he did not consider the monopolistic trading policy of France. Scarcely had the post been established, when his Royal Majesty handed it over to the Company of the Colony,[15] which in 1700 had superseded the Company of the Domain.[16] Great must have been Cadillac's chagrin thus to see others calmly assume possession of what he had taken so much pains to establish. To crown it all, on July 18, 1702, he was ordered to proceed to Montreal and Quebec to make arrangements with the very men who were to rob him of the fruit of his labor.[17] However, he surrendered the control of the post, and the period of the Company's rule began.

Hampered and restricted was the system of trade they introduced at Detroit. Peltry traffic must be confined within the boundaries of the fort.[18] Officers, soldiers, and settlers must not participate in this precious fur trade, for the Company sent "two upright men" to take charge of it for His Majesty.[19] The

13. *Mich. Hist. Colls.*, XXXIII, 97; see also *Jes. Rel.*, LXV, 273.
14. *Mich. Hist. Colls.*, XXIX, 270; XXXIII, 152.
15. *Ibid*, XXXIII, 204.
16. Margry, *Déc. et étab.*, V, 172-3, 360-1; *Mich. Hist. Colls.*, XXIX, 270-1. *Jes. Rel.*, LXV, 273. The Company of the colony of Canada, by a decree of the king's council of state, were permitted to sell, trade, etc., all beaver skins, beginning in 1699, on paying one-fourth in kind of said beaver to the Farmers of the Western Domain.
17. *N. Y. Col. Docs.*, IX, 805-8; *Mich. Hist. Colls.*, XXXIII, 204.
18. *Mich. Hist. Colls.*, XXXIII, 156.
19. *Ibid*, 109.

beaver pelt must be left strictly alone, as markets had more beaver than they could use.[20] Such were their stipulations as to trade. To the king they promised to pay the six thousand pounds he wanted for the relief of poor families of this country, and to assume all expenses he had incurred at the post including those of goods sent for trading purposes, on condition that such expenses should not exceed fifteen thousand pounds.[21] To Cadillac whom they retained in their services, they first agreed to grant one-third of the trade, but later he was given a stipend of two thousand pounds, annually, while Sir de Tonty, his assistant, was to have two-thirds as much.[22]

Cadillac had promised the company to suppress the beaver hunt, and according to his own statement this was done. There was no restriction as to other classes of furred animals,[23] so the savages were engaged in hunting for the skins of elk, stags, roebucks, otters, black bears, and other furs. As they were able to supply their wants by the trade they carried on in

20.   *Ibid*, 108, 152-3; Parkman, *Old Régime*, 307-8.
21.   *Mich. Hist. Colls.*, XXXIII, 109.
22.   *Ibid*, 157.
23.   *Ibid*, 168. That the market was overstocked with beaver and hence licenses revoked, has already been mentioned, also the fact that this was largely due to the extent to which trade was being pushed in the New World. Parkman refers to another cause; he says there was less demand for beaver, as hatters reduced the size of hats and mixed rabbit fur with the beaver.—Parkman, *Old Régime*, 307. When the new company was formed in 1700, they took from the hands of the former company an accumulation of 600,000 pounds of beaver, paying only one-half the usual price. French markets refused to buy; hence the directors burned three-fourths, and to rid themselves of what remained they begged the king to issue a decree requiring hatters to put at least three ounces of beaver into each hat.—*Ibid*, 308.

those skins, they had by 1702 largely given up hunting the beaver, so that this trade at Detroit had not exceeded ten thousand skins, as appeared from the receipt of the warehouse keepers.[24] In his letter to Count Pontchartrain August 31, 1703, Cadillac states that not more than eight thousand had been sent out from there, the surplus trade being large skins and small furs.[25] An attempt to handle the pelts of the buffalo did not prove a success, as the company held forth no inducement for prosecuting such a plan.   Six francs each was all that was offered for them, which would hardly pay a hunter for lugging a package of two hundred and fifty to three hundred pounds from three to four leagues inland, as long as beaver skins were so much lighter and easier to transport. So the lazy Indian was ready to abandon the chase for the buffalo, as soon as other furs could be obtained.[26]

But in spite of their system of monopoly, exclusion, and restriction of the beaver hunt, trade did not seem to prosper under the Company's régime. Various things may account for this, perhaps not the least of which was the personnel of the Company and their method of conducting business. Cadillac calls them a beggarly set, far from versed in the management of a frontier trading post in the wilderness; two, lawyers skilled only in drawing up deeds; and the others, merchants who knew little beyond selling to advantage and whose private affairs, even, were not in the best of condition.[27] That theirs was not an enlightened

24. *Mich. Hist. Colls.*, XXXIII, 144.
25. Letter of Pontchartrain, in Sheldon, *Hist. of Mich.*, 115.
26. Sheldon, *Hist. of Mich.*, 106-7.
27. *Mich. Hist. Colls.*, XXXIII, 179-80; 153-5; XXIX, 271.
     They were not fully in sympathy with Cadillac who was

policy of trade is certain, but such was French policy everywhere in the New World, and it is highly probable that Cadillac presented in somewhat unfavorable light men who had become masters where he had hoped to reign supreme. Then, too, considerable friction was rife among the managers at Detroit. The clerks of the Company had charge of the store house. They refused to obey Cadillac's orders and complained against him. He was ordered to Montreal, placed under arrest, and detained for some time.[28] Restriction of the beaver trade for the less lucrative commerce in other furs, and the competition of the English with their cheaper merchandise and higher prices for peltries, no doubt helped to diminish the prosperity of the post in these early years of its existence.

Cadillac questions the possibility of the Company's loss being as great as they tried to make it appear. They seemed disgusted with the post, because, they said, they lost in trade by it.[29] They had sent him an account showing a deficit of twelve thousand two hundred and ninety-seven pounds and seventeen shillings, according to their figures. But evidently their arithmetic and Cadillac's did not agree for he found in it a gain of twenty thousand.[30] Riverin's report for the first year showed ten thousand

---

27. *Con.* looking forward to colonizing this section. Mr. Burton, in his *Fort Pontchartrain du Detroit* says that the Board of directors at Montreal were higher colonial officials related to one another, whose income was almost exclusively from the fur trade and selling of congés, hence they were opposed to settlement. *Mich. Hist. Colls.*, XXIX, 271.
28. *Ibid*, XXIX, 271.
29. *Ibid*, XXXIII, 179.
30. *Ibid*.

four hundred ninety-four pounds worth of beaver
skins in the Detroit accounts; and for the second,
eighteen thousand two hundred and thirty-nine; i. e.,
twenty-eight thousand, seven hundred and thirty-three
pounds worth in two years, or an average of fourteen
thousand three hundred and sixty-six pounds, and
ten shillings for each year. Considering that the
company was to furnish its agents no more than one
hundred fifty thousand pounds worth annually, some
estimate of Detroit's share in the whole trade can be
formed.[31] However, the amount of fur sold is scarcely
an indication of a gain, or loss, in times when the post
was struggling against many odds.

It is reasonable to suppose that the company was
really losing in trade. Had it been otherwise, they
would never have given up the post in days like those,
when the fur trade was the very food and life of the
Canadian province. One thing is certain, they were
weary of their undertaking. Complaints were made
to Count Pontchartrain,[32] who laid the matter before
the king. Cadillac offered to take charge of the post,
so His Majesty asked the directors of the Company to
place it in his hands, and commanded him to go to
Quebec, that arrangements might be made for such
a transfer.[33] This was done, and September 28, 1705,
Cadillac at last became chief in command of the post
he had founded.[34] He claims that he found it in

31. *Ibid*, 185.
32. In a letter of Louis XIV to the Canadian officials May 30,
    1703, he states that the Company claimed it involved
    them in exorbitant expense, beyond their power to sustain.
    N. Y. Col. Docs., IX, 742; *Wis. Hist. Colls.*, XVI, 218.
33. *Mich. Hist. Colls.*, XXXIII, 187.
34. *Ibid*, 245-8.

wretched condition, a large portion of peltries rotten and spoiled, and the Company's store pillaged.[35]

Experience had taught the Company of the Colony no lesson. They had yet to learn that restriction of trade was detrimental to the progress of any trading post, for their terms of agreement with Cadillac September 28, 1705, smacked strongly of French monopoly. No more than fifteen or twenty thousand livres worth of beaver skins annually were to be paid for by them. Cadillac and his people were commanded to confine trade strictly within the limits of the colony. They were to send no agents into remote districts and no trading boats to Michilimackinac. They were to sit quietly at home and wait for the manna to drop into their laps. One thing they could do. They were permitted to entice to Detroit every red man in Michigan if they were able to do so.[36]

And that is just what Cadillac attempted to do. Vigorously he set to work to build up the little Indian settlement around his post. Little cared he where the savage came from, or by what means he was brought. It might mean the desertion of posts already in existence, but that could not be helped. Without the Indian the fur commerce did not flourish, and on this rude frontier, with the existing policy of trade, the strongest alone could survive. His efforts were, evidently, crowned with success, for Michili-mackinac was almost abandoned, and Huron, Ottawas, and Pottawatomi assembled at Detroit, until, according to Cadillac, two thousand Indians were gathered

35. *Wis. Hist. Colls.*, XVI, 243.
36. *Mich. Hist. Colls.*, XXXIII, 245-8, 187-9.

there, even some Iroquois coming and making it their home.[37]

Royal decrees against the liquor traffic caused Cadillac little uneasiness. It was said that fifteen barrels of brandy were carried with him to Detroit and three hundred livres weight more were to be sent later.[38] This is not at all unlikely, for he held that some liquor was absolutely necessary to keep the loyalty of their Indian allies, as coureurs de bois and English traders were more than willing and ever ready to quench the thirst of the Indians. So Cadillac permitted the traffic, and governor and intendant as far as the liquor deal was concerned saw not, neither did they hear.[39] Two factors governed Cadillac's policy. He was aiming first to preserve trade by holding the allegiance of the Indians, and secondly to prevent drunkenness. To this end he caused all liquor to be placed in the store house, and sold to each in his turn. Whoever wanted a drink, must get it there, and he doled it out in such exasperatingly small amounts as a twenty-fourth part of a quart; just a mere taste, that there might be no possibility of intoxication on the part of any one.[40]

Considering that fur was the all-important thing in early days, the medium of exchange entering into a variety of business transactions, it is not strange that limitations and restrictions placed upon trade at

37. *Ibid*, VIII, 429; XXXIII, 207.
38. *N. Y. Col. Docs.*, IX, 807; *Wis. Hist. Colls.*, XVI, 245; *Mich. Hist. Colls.*, XXIX, 301.
39. *Wis. Hist. Colls.*, XVI, 253.
40. *Ibid.* According to Thwaites, "quart" here indicates "a small cask containing not a quarter, but about half as much as a cask of ordinary size." *Wis. Hist. Colls.*, XVI, 253n.

Detroit should have caused considerable trouble, and that fraud and illicit traffic should have crept in. M. de Tonty and two clerks were caught trading, though bound by contract not to do so, and were accused of taking from the warehouse goods amounting to fourteen thousand livres. Likewise the two commissioners, Armand and Nolan were detected in the embezzlement of furs.[41] These were the bigger thieves. Undoubtedly there were many others, who in a smaller way and on a smaller scale, transgressed rules and commands, since the beaver pelt was so temptingly near and the hand of authority so far removed. Even Cadillac, chief of the post, who as such should have been a shining example following closely the terms of agreement, proved a transgressor.[42] How he treated decrees pertaining to the liquor traffic has already been pointed out; but that was not his only sin, according to M. D'Aigremont. The Company of the Colony when turning over Detroit to Cadillac, retained the right of sending an inspector.[43] Rumors of excessive brandy sale and other transgressions at this post had reached the ears of the king, and His Royal Highness sent M. D'Aigremont to the western posts on a tour of inspection.[44] He accused Cadillac of illegal trade, even of carrying furs to the English. He

41. *Mich. Hist. Colls.*, XXXIII, 209.
42. Cadillac claimed that his warning the Company against the two clerks led to their accusation against him. *Ibid*, XXXIII, 209.

Mr. Burton states that Cadillac himself did not engage in trading with the Indians but was contented with his other income. *Mich. Hist. Colls.*, XXIX, 301.
43. *Ibid*, XXXIII, 345-6.
44. *N. Y. Col. Docs.*, IX, 807; *Wis. Hist. Colls.*, XVI, 245; *Mich. Hist. Colls.*, XXIX, 301.

states that even if one-tenth of the savages of Canada should come to Detroit there would not be one-tenth the return of the number of beaver skins that there might be at Michilimackinac under similar conditions, for they would be sent to the English through the Iroquois.[45] Too much credence however can not be attached to D'Aigremont's view of the matter, for he favored the re-establishment of Michilimackinac and, naturally, would put forth every argument in its favor; besides, according to Cadillac, he tarried too short a time at the post to see and understand its actual condition, seeking information concerning it among Cadillac's enemies. Evidently the king was satisfied that conditions were not as bad as depicted, for he simply left matters in Cadillac's hands.[46]

Trade was not quite as close a monopoly during Cadillac's régime as under that of the Company, for he permitted the inhabitants to trade, on condition that they pay a small tax; in one of his grants of land, this provision is noted, that the grantee may trade, hunt, and fish, provided he pay five livres for that right. No doubt, the majority availed themselves of this privilege which gave them a hand in the fur trade.[47]

Cadillac's labors at Detroit did not cover a wide span of years. On September 11, 1710, after guiding the affairs of his little post for only seven years, in which the colony and the trade were fairly prosperous, he was sent, much to his chagrin, as governor to Louisiana, and another commandant assumed control.[48]

45. *Wis. Hist. Colls.*, XVI, 255-6; Sheldon, *Hist. of Mich.*, 280-94.
46. *N. Y. Col. Docs.*, IX, 827.
47. Farmer, *Hist. of Detroit*, 18; *Wis. Hist. Colls.*, XVI, 254.
48. Brymner, *Canadian Archives*, 1899 (Sup.), 436.

From now on until the close of the French régime the post passed from hand to hand, its trading fortunes depending on and varying with its masters; some of these mere substitutes tarried but a short time; others not much longer, as they were removed for reasons best known to themselves and their employers; hence their period of rule was of little significance and may be dismissed with mere notice. But that of men like Sir de la Forest and Alphonse de Tonty was of more importance, covering a longer period and having greater effect upon trade.

Sir de la Forest, old veteran in the service of Canada and the fur trade, was named as Cadillac's successor. His privileges and duties were similar to those of his predecessor. First of all, he was forbidden to trade in brandy and to allow its sale under any circumstances whatsoever. He had strict injunctions to shut out all British merchandise and permit no beaver pelt to find its way into their territory, and Indians must be permitted to go to Michilimackinac to trade if they so desired.[49]

Unable because of ill health to take command of the post, he at once sent his agent, M. Dubuisson, in his place.[50] Whatever else may be said of the latter, his courage did not fail him, for he calmly took posession of Cadillac's belongings, movable and otherwise, and monopolized revenues and profits, in fact, the entire commerce, excluding from trade all those who formerly enjoyed trading rights.[51] Cadillac strongly protested against having his property thus swallowed up, property

49. *Ibid.*
50. *Mich. Hist. Colls.*, XXXIV, 310.
51. *Ibid*, XXXIII, 507, 508-9.

which according to his own estimation was worth thirty thousand livres; but Dubuisson was deaf to all protests and attempts at compromise. So there was nothing left for the former commandant to do but to appeal to headquarters. Finally, July 3, 1711, he made an agreement with De la Forest, whereby two officers, named by Cadillac, were to be in command at Detroit until the following year, to take care of his property and trade for his profit. A certain amount of goods had already been sent to the post by De la Forest, so it was agreed that they might be used, but no more were to be bought by him in the future for the Indian trade. If Cadillac still had goods in Detroit the following year, he was to sell them to De la Forest, or have them taken away at his own expense.[52]

But De la Forest soon found a pretext to break the agreement. "As I bear the expense," said he, "how can Cadillac take it into his head that I would let him carry on the trading? Since it pleased His Majesty to give me the command of Detroit, and the trade, it is fair that I should enjoy them, as I have always done until now."[53] So in spite of Cadillac and all he could say and do to the contrary, De la Forest proceeded to the post, claiming that Indian disturbances demanded his immediate presence there.[54] When he arrived he took complete possession of all trade, as had Dubuisson before him;[55] but his trading career was short; in 1714 he died,[56] and M. de Sabrevois

52.   *Ibid*, 510-11.
53.   Adapted from *Ibid*, 516.
54.   *Ibid*, 512.
55.   *Wis. Hist. Colls.*, XVI, 308, 310; *N. Y. Col. Docs.*, IX, 866-7.
56.   *Mich. Hist. Colls.*, XXXIII, 572.

was sent to take his place.[57]   M. de Sabrevois, unlike
the other commandants, was not permitted to trade,
and already in 1717, the post was taken from him and
given to Alphonse de Tonty;[58] the license system had
been restored in 1716, but this did not affect Detroit,
for, as a rule, trade there was left in the commandant's
hands.[59]

Much dissatisfaction and abuse in trade characterized
the administration of Alphonse de Tonty.   Apparently
his intentions at first were good, for he began his career
by making trade free to all, but he became involved
in debt.   In his extremity he bethought himself of
another plan, namely, that of farming out his privileges
to two men, François la Marque and Louis Gastineau.
These were to have the exclusive trade of the place
on the condition that they pay him an annuity.[60]
Some trouble arose which soon severed this partnership.   Then Tonty leased the privilege to three others,
who formed an association of trade with La Marque
and Gastineau.[61]

But the citizens of Detroit were not to be imposed
upon thus and have their precious fur trade sold to
whoever had means to buy it.   They rose in rebellion
and drew up a petition, voicing their grievances against
this Nero of the Western World.   It seems rather
curious that any protest should have been made against
subletting the monopoly of trade, unless the idea was
that one tyrant was more desirable than four or five.
Doubtless, had that been the commandant's only

57.   *Ibid*, XXXIV, 312.
58.   *Ibid*.
59.   *Wis. Hist. Colls.*, XVIII, 26n.
60.   *Mich. Hist. Colls.*, XXXIV, 314.
61.   *Ibid*.

misdeed, little, perhaps nothing, would have been said.
But evidently other sins lay at his door. Cruelty
and injustice were the charges heading the list of
accusations against him. If the petitioners wished
to go to Detroit, he made them purchase a license for
which five hundred pounds worth of skins, Detroit
price, had to be paid. He was usually party and judge
to all difficulties about trading, caring for nothing
save his own interests.[62] But that was not all. Boats
obliged to winter in other posts or settlements drew
their provisions from Detroit, but this was no longer
an advantage, for Tonty forbade the inhabitants to
sell their corn and enjoined hawkers not to buy from
them. As to brandy, not a single drop must be sold,
for that was against the decrees of the king. The
petitioners had given credit to some of the savages, no
doubt, during the first part of Tonty's régime, when
trade was free to all, and now he forbade their leaving
the fort; but he, himself, loaded his boats with merchandise and went to the various hunting grounds, securing
all the skins, so that nothing was left for them.[63] The
Huron Indians, who likewise entered a complaint, told
the same story. They grumbled much, because now
there was only one trading house at Detroit, while
formerly there had been several. The owners of this
post, said they, came out several leagues, met the
hunters, charged their own price for the merchandise,
and took from them all the furs, giving the Detroit
settlers no hand whatever in the bargain.[64]

French authorities received and considered the

62. *Ibid*, 38; XXXIII, 707-9.
63. *Ibid*, XXXIII, 707-9.
64. *Ibid*, XXXIV, 49-51. See merchants' complaint, *Ibid*,
        XXXIII, 708.

complaints against Tonty. But they felt that too much faith could not be placed in the testimony of the Huron, for the cunning Indian was an apt pupil who could glibly recite a story told him if it might prove of some advantage. The authorities emphatically denied any right on the part of Tonty to try to control the movements of the settlers and prevent them from carrying on general trade. His monopoly was to extend to the fur trade and that alone. If he wished to sublet his rights, that was his business and it could not be considered a wrong.[65]

In the summer of 1730 Sieur de Boishebert went to Detroit as commandant. Under him, permits were granted, as he preferred to do no trading himself. However, such expenses as would be incurred for interpreter and for buying Indian presents were assumed by him. That pleased the voyageur and, according to Hocquart and Beauharnois, a greater number than usual went up, so that goods for the Indian trade became cheaper.[66]

By 1738 the Hurons and Ottawas clashed, and trade languished.[67] The commandant was forbidden to pursue the peltry trade; his remuneration was supposed to come from the sale of licenses. The number of permits granted for Detroit trade, according to Hocquart and Beauharnois, was not limited, and residents of that place obtained the privilege of trade for the asking, on the same condition as voyageurs.[68] De Noyan claimed that traders were far too numerous

65. *Ibid*, XXXIV, 55-59.
66. *Wis. Hist. Colls.*, XVII, 133-4; *Mich. Hist. Colls.*, XXXIV, 87.
67. *Wis. Hist. Colls.*, XVII, 326-7, 328, 340-5.
68. *Ibid*, 297.

to flourish, as they ruined each other by underselling,
bringing goods below cost, so that they were unable
to meet their engagements with Montreal merchants.
Their goods and houses were sold every day, says he,
until the Montreal merchants had more mortgages
in Detroit than Detroit was worth.[69]

From the earliest times, the British trader had been
a constant menace to the French. Each year he
seemed to encroach more and more upon their territory.
Sieur de Céloron who succeeded Noyan at Detroit,
in 1742, was commanded to take the strictest care
that no outsiders, only French settlers and voyageurs,
were permitted to trade.[70] A desperate effort had
been made by France to keep out English goods and
prevent Englishmen from getting a single beaver pelt
on their lands; but where so many diverse elements
were present,—the coureur de bois, who cared little
where he sold his pelts, just so he was well paid; the
fickle Indian to whom cheap trinkets and brandy were
big temptations; and commandants with patriotic
fervor less strong than love for gain,—this was almost
a hopeless task.[71] Hostile Indians, incited by the
English, took sides, warring with one another and
playing havoc with the fur trade. Detroit, surrounded
by savage tribes, was in the very center of this Indian
warfare. So it is not surprising that trade was fast
falling off. In 1745 fewer goods were brought to the

69. *Ibid*, 326.
70. Letter of Beauharnois to French Minister, *Ibid*, XVII, 415.
     The French and voyageurs were also to have the privilege
     of trading at Grosse Isle, if they wished. *Ibid*.
71. The English were constantly luring the Indians away and
     usurping French trade. *Ibid*, XVI, 256-7; *Ibid*, XVII,
     358, 446-7; *N. Y. Col. Docs.*, X, 21; *Mich. Hist. Colls.*,
     XXXIV, 103, 88.
7

post than formerly. Merchandise was high and peltries were low. Licenses were offered for nothing to induce voyageurs to go there, but in spite of this, Beauharnois tells us, only ten were willing to go.[72] In the following year, of the twelve licenses offered there was only one for which five hundred livres were paid. The other eleven remained unsold. "It was all we could do," said Hocquart and Beauharnois, "to Engage Voyageurs, in consideration of the full remission of the price of the License and of the obligation to Transport the munitions required for the service."[73]

Protection against the Indians and their allies was a question forcing itself to the forefront to the exclusion of trade.[74] The French and Indian War was at hand, and for a few years to come the furred animals of Michigan forests were to rest in peace while their enemies were killing each other.

No mention has been made of the individual trader, and little need be said, for the day of the independent, individual trader had not arrived. Trade was in the hands of one man, or company. Cadillac, as has already been pointed out, granted the privilege of trade to settlers for a small tax. Tonty sublet the monopoly, but only to a few. Toward the close of the French régime, the privilege of trade was extended

---

72. *N. Y. Col. Docs.*, X, 21; *Wis. Hist. Colls.*, XVII, 450.
   The savages were refusing to hunt as they were not supplied with enough brandy. *Mich. Hist. Colls.*, XXXIV, 102.
73. Letters of Beauharnois and Hocquart to French Minister, *Wis. Hist. Colls.*, XVII, 450.
74. Longueil was planning to send that summer four hundred Canadians to Detroit to go to other posts and winter nearest the enemy, while next spring he intended to send five or six hundred more.—*N. Y. Col. Docs.*, X, 251, and 137-145.

to any citizen of Detroit, on the same condition as to voyageurs; but then there was less time and opportunity for trade, as the Indians were bent on war and deserted their hunting pursuits.

Father Richardie, in his report on the Detroit Huron mission, mentions a Sieur Carignan, trader at Detroit; also a Sieur Gouin.[75] No doubt, all the settlers dealt more or less in peltries, for they were a medium of exchange. In referring to the above mentioned reports, it will be seen how the debts to the good Father were discharged by means of furs, either beaver or small furs;[76] in 1742 Jacques Campau was to pay him for a number of items in peltries, at Detroit prices;[77] Madame de la Forest owed him thirty-one beaver skins, the balance of what he sold her the previous year;[78] he loaned Baptiste Piponnette twenty-one livres, which were to be returned to him in small skins;[79] and July 20th, 1745, he sent to a merchant in Montreal, six hundred raccoon skins, fifty-seven otter, and seventeen lynx. The five packs sent, he says, were covered with nine large castors and a rare deer skin.[80] Fur was the money of the day, an item entering into every-day life. So though the trade was largely in the hands of the commandant, exchange of fur was, no doubt, a common thing in every household of Detroit during the French régime.

75.   *Jes. Rel.*, LXX, 35.
76.   Report of Detroit Mission, *Ibid*, LXIX, 241-277; LXX, 21-77.
77.   *Ibid*, LXIX, 247.
78.   *Ibid*, 249.
79.   *Ibid*, 261.
80.   *Ibid*.

CHAPTER III

REVIVAL OF MICHILIMACKINAC AND OTHER POSTS

THE rise of Detroit proved a death blow to Michilimackinac and her trade, for, accepting the invitation extended by Cadillac to every savage tribe within reach to join the Indian settlement at Detroit, Huron and Ottawa deserted the old post for the new.[1] The king, must have favored this plan, for Royal instructions went forth that no commandant be appointed at Michilimackinac in order that the Indians might be compelled to go to Detroit.[2] Not such was the attitude of Governor General and intendant, according to Cadillac, for he claimed that they with the Jesuits did all in their power to keep them away.[3] Doubtless, Etienne Carheil, the Jesuit priest of Michilimackinac, who had brought down upon himself the enmity and wrath of Cadillac and the fur traders, largely by his bitter opposition to the brandy traffic,[4] strongly resented and opposed this wholesale migration of Huron and Ottawa to the Lower Peninsula. Whether the savage was willing and happy to go has been

1. *Mich. Hist. Colls.*, VIII, 429; Margry, *Déc. et étab.* V, 201-3.
2. Brymner, *Canadian Archives*, 1899 (Sup.), 207. By 1706, soldiers and commandants had been recalled from most of the upper posts.—*Wis. Hist. Colls.*, XVI, 230 (n.2).
3. *Mich. Hist. Colls.*, XXXIII, 204.
4. *Jes. Rel.*, L, 325n.

questioned; nevertheless, he went.[5] Fur was king.
His love for and devotion to the forest commerce were
stronger than his piety, so that by 1703 Etienne
Carheil was forced to leave, as his little flock had
deserted him for Cadillac and the fur trade of Detroit.[6]

What a gloomy picture the good priest gives of
Michilimackinac. According to him, at the opening
of the eighteenth century it was a resort for gamblers
and drunkards, and a den of lawlessness and fraud,
of wickedness and vice.[7] In the good old days, says
he, the missionary had some influence with the trader;
now he had none, for the latter realized that no matter
what he might do, the commandants would uphold
him.[8] What havoc soldiers and commandants wrought
at the post. They impaired both the advancement
of faith and the trade of the voyageurs.[9] Though they
had come to uphold the law, they themselves violated
it on every hand. Forbidden to trade, yet they
traded. The soldiers roamed through the forest selling
merchandise and brandy to the Indians, sharing the
profits with the commandant. At the post, open
liquor shops were maintained, where drunken Indians,
soldiers, coureurs de bois, commandants, and licensed
traders drank, gambled, and made merry, day and
night; the latter imitating, at times surpassing, the

5. Some hold that at first they favored the migration to Detroit,
    thinking it might help to destroy their enemies, the
    Iroquois. When they saw this was not the outcome, they
    were disappointed. *Jes. Rel.*, LXV, 18-21, 189, 253;
    See also, *N. Y. Col. Docs.*, IX, 750-51; *Wis. Hist. Colls.*,
    XVI, 235-8.
6. *Jes. Rel.*, L, 325.
7. *Jes. Rel.*, LXV, 191.
8. *Ibid*, 203-5.
9. *Ibid*, 195.

savagery, coarseness, and barbarism of their Indian allies.[10] Then, too, these men had taught the Indian a bad habit, in buying his good will and service with presents. Now the red man expected a gift for every little service rendered, and would do nothing without it.[11] With such a state of affairs, it is not strange that Father Carheil recommended a return to the policy of early days, when the savage brought his peltries directly to Montreal.[12]

Though Indians, Jesuit priest, commandant and soldiers had departed, to say that Michilimackinac was wholly abandoned would be false. M. d'Aigremont, who was there on a tour of inspection in 1708, relates that the place was occupied by a few wanderers, fourteen or fifteen Frenchmen, who could not possibly live if Montreal merchants did not send them goods.[13] These were coureurs de bois, who rendered the colony a valuable service by bringing from here to Montreal many peltries, which would otherwise have gone to the English; but who caused Cadillac considerable worry, by smuggling in liquor, and luring back the savages from Detroit.[14] D'Aigremont claimed that these men were not the only traders at Michilimackinac, as many canoes went up, pretending they were in government service, but really loaded with goods for the Indian trade.[15] That his statement is true is highly probable, for numerous instances of illicit

10. *Ibid*, 195-205.
11. *Ibid*, 215-16.
12. *Ibid*, 219.
13. Summary of Inspection, *Wis. Hist. Colls.*, XVI, 259; Sheldon, *Hist. of Mich.*, 280-94.
14. *Wis. Hist. Colls.*, XVI, 297, 259; *Ibid*, XVIII, 80-1; *N. Y. Col. Docs.*, IX, 852.
15. Summary of Inspection. *Wis. Hist. Colls.*, XVI, 259.

trade by Colonial officials and their agents are mentioned in the early history of the Canadian province.[16]

This was too favorable a spot for trade to be abandoned for any length of time. By 1712 the number of coureurs de bois who made this their rendezvous had increased to forty;[17] and the story goes, that the following year one hundred Frenchmen came up, secretly traded away the goods of merchants who had fitted them out, and then escaped to the Mississippi establishment.[18] D'Aigremont, in his report on western posts, recommended that something be done to preserve Michilimackinac trade. So steps were taken for its re-establishment[19] and Sieur M. Louvigny was ordered to go there and gather together the savages.[20] This was not an easy task, because Queen Anne's War was in progress and considerable unrest prevailed among them. The Renards were attacking the Ottawas and hampering the fur trade,[21] so little could be done until the close of the war, when this upper post was again established.

To enlist the services of the coureurs de bois in quelling the Indian wars, it was suggested in 1713-14 that licenses for trade be offered to them,[22] and in 1716 the license system revoked in 1696 was again restored. Licenses countersigned by the intendant were to be granted to poor families whom the Governor

16. *N. Y. Col. Docs.*, IX, 159-60, 152-55, 141-2.
17. Memorial of Intendant, *Wis. Hist. Colls.*, XVI, 295, 297.
18. Letter of Ramezay and Bégon, *Ibid*, 331.
19. Summary of Inspection, *Ibid*, 257-8; see also 296-7.
20. *Wis. Hist. Colls.*, XVI, 295-6.
21. *Ibid*, 299; XVII, 100-2.
22. *Wis. Hist. Colls.*, XVI, 299.

judged most needy.   If too poor to make use of them
they might sell them to others.[23]   Twenty-five permits
were to be granted annually by the Governor General
of New France and the holder of such a permit must
trade within the post designated.[24]   The aim was to
prevent the disorders that formerly occurred when
voyageurs were permitted to go wherever they pleased
to trade.[25]   The country was divided into districts
and the traders were not to go beyond the limits of
the one assigned, nor carry any more liquor with them
than was necessary for their own use, as they were not
to sell any to the Indians.   Under these regulations
canoes were to proceed first to the main post of their
particular district, and from there the voyageurs departed for the hunting grounds.[26]   "Voyageurs who
went to the upper country readily submitted," said
Governor Vaudreuil, "since each one found it to his advantage" to do so.[27]   To dispose of licenses for Michilimackinac   trade,   however,   was   found   difficult,   as
Monsieur de Louvigny was glad to offer men free
passage and liberty to trade provided they joined his
forces against the Indians.[28]

23.   Letter from Gov. Vaudreuil to Minister, *Ibid*, XVI, 437;
        see also *Wis. Hist. Colls.*, XVIII, 26.
24.   *Ibid*.
25.   *Ibid;* see also 388.
26.   *Ibid*, XVIII, 290.   "The king's Posts or rather the In-
        tendant's were the only ones excepted from this general
        Rule."   *Ibid*.
27.   Letter from Gov. Vaudreuil to Minister, *Ibid*, XVI, 437-8,
        see also p. 388.
28.   *Wis. Hist. Colls.*, XVI, 330.   Sieur de Ramezay and Sieur
        de Bégon in writing to the French ministers in 1715 state,
        that it would be impossible for them to sell any licenses
        the following year, as men could go to the Upper Peninsula
        without them.   Even if they could find some one to

Chief among the Indian tribes who traded at this post were the Saulteux and Ottawas.[29] As a rule most of the Indians in this section were friends of the French, but they were filled with a certain fear and awe of the English. When the latter could not coax or force them to bring their peltries, they tried to frighten them to do so. A curious story is told which shows how the ignorance and superstition of the red man was made use of by them. British traders sent collars to a certain Indian tribe and forbade them on penalty of death to carry their furs to any one but them. The Indians did not follow the behests of the English, and when about eight hundred of their number died from cold they were stricken with fear, as they thought that the Great Spirit had punished them for their disobedience.[30] In such wise, by fair means or foul, Englishmen were able to secure part of the trade claimed by the French. But if they had to frighten the Indians to get their furs, such means were not necessary with some traders, who were ever ready and anxious to accept English goods and brandy. Resourceful in finding excuses, these men claimed that this was their only way to obtain credits which they had granted for loans. Such misdemeanors had to be dealt with, so French officials clapped on another ordinance to their already long list of orders and decrees, and forbade all such foreign commerce on penalty of confiscation of their goods and a fine of five hundred livres.[31]

---

28. *Con.* purchase them, it would be on the condition that they have entire liberty to carry on trade and not be obliged to join Louvigny's forces.—*Ibid.*
29. Memoir of Bougainville, *Wis. Hist. Colls.*, XVIII, 183.
30. Brymner, *Canadian Archives*, 1886, clxv.
31. Ordinance on Fur Trade, *Wis. Hist. Colls.*, XVII, 214-15.

After her re-establishment, Michilimackinac regained her prominence as a trading center but slowly. This was not strange for it took some time to get the Indians back and accustom them to again bring their peltries thither. Though more of the wilderness was open for trade, at the same time competitive posts had arisen. A more powerful factor, however, in hindering the forest commerce, was war, both inter-tribal and inter-colonial. There was considerable trouble in all of the posts in the late forties because of war, but this section seemed particularly to be in a turmoil.[32] Some Frenchmen were killed at Sanguinon, an Ottawa village between Detroit and Michilimackinac, others at La Cloche, others at Grosse Isle, and some within the very post itself. Mr. de St. Pierre, who was sent there to bring order out of chaos, detained all voyageurs with their goods at the post, and threatened the Indians that unless the murderers were brought to justice no traders would be sent among them.[33] This had the desired effect, for the Indians had become dependent on the white man and were as anxious to obtain his trinkets, as he was to get their peltries. To say that it put an end to all such disturbances and made the life of the traders secure would be untrue, for such a state of affairs under the existing circumstances, in such troublous times, was impossible.

War not only endangered the life of the trader, but lessened and made unprofitable his trade, so that it was difficult to get men to engage in it. In 1746 only five licenses were issued for the post and nothing

32. Gov. and Intendant's Diary of Events. *Wis. Hist. Colls.*, XVII, 462-5; see also pp. 470 and 508. *N. Y. Col. Docs.*, X, 119-20.
33. *Wis. Hist. Colls.*, XVII, 509; *N. Y., Col. Docs.*, X, 119, 183.

was paid for them.[34]   The following year ten canoes went up, nine of which paid four hundred livres each, on condition that each carry eight hundred weight for the king. The tenth paid seven hundred but carried nothing.[35]   In 1757 the post was exploited by licenses costing six hundred francs per canoe, and each was obliged to carry five hundred weight for officers and garrisons. From six to seven hundred packs were sent from the place yearly.[36]

It was natural as the frontier line of trade advanced and little posts sprang up farther on in the wilderness, that at first they should be little outposts of the older ones.   In 1748 Sieur La Galissonière recommended that all posts called northern, as La Baye and those on Lake Superior, be made subordinate to Michilimackinac, but nothing was done at the time.[37] In 1746, the commandant had looked after the first named post, sending two men there with outfits on the condition that they pay him one thousand livres each.   But evidently it was not satisfactory, as it was said that the commandant provided but indifferently for the trade.[38]

Besides the northern posts another region came directly under the supervision of this place, namely Grand River Valley.   In October, 1755 Louis Herbin, the commandant there, sent De Langlade to that

---

34. Beauharnois and Hocquart to French Minister, *Wis. Hist. Colls.*, XVII, 450.
35. *Wis. Hist. Colls.*, XVII, 471-2.   Galissonière and Hocquart to French Minister.
36. Memoir of Bougainville, *Wis. Hist. Colls.*, XVIII, 183.
37. La Galissonière to French Minister, *Wis. Hist. Colls.*, XVII, 501.
38. Beauharnois and Hocquart to French Minister, *Wis. Hist. Colls.*, XVII, 450-51.

place to take command of the whole of Grand River and dependency, locating his establishment at a place called Gabagouache. He was ordered to leave the Kalamazoo River trade free for all who wished to go there for that purpose, and was expressly forbidden under penalty of punishment from going to trade in any other place whatsoever. He was to see that his traders and hired men were not absent without permission, and the latter must present themselves to him before going hunting, no doubt that he might see what they carried with them to the hunting grounds. Moreover, he must see that one trader did not interfere with the trade of another.[39]

Considering the important location of the Sault on the highway to northern trade, it seems strange that for such a long time no effort was made to re-establish the post abandoned in 1689. A few Indians made it their home,[40] and voyageurs may have tarried there a short time on their journey farther westward, for in 1747 a number of these were robbed and mal-treated there.[41] No permanent reoccupation is heard of again, until Sieur La Jonquière, in 1750, sent Sieur Chevalier de Repentigny to forestall the attempt made by the English to secure the trade and allegiance of the savages of the northern posts through messages, presents, and by other means. The post was to be a hereditary seigniory; he was to establish it at his own expense, building a stockaded fort; he was also to cultivate the soil and raise stock for the traders of Lake Superior. Trade was to be free to the com-

39.   Langlade Papers, *Wis. Hist. Colls.*, VIII, 211.
40.   *Wis. Hist. Colls.*, XVIII, 99n.
41.   *N. Y. Col. Docs.*, X, 183.

mandant but the post subordinate to that of Michilimackinac.[42] The Saulteux were the chief Indians
trading there and it is thought that about a hundred
packs were sent from the post annually.[43] Considerable
trouble, however, was experienced with the Indians
because they carried their furs to the English, who
loaded them with presents, so that in 1751 Repentigny
forbade the savages of his post to winter at Saguinau,
which formed a stepping stone into the lands of the
English.[44]

From the time when La Salle's fort at the mouth
of St. Joseph River was abandoned, there seems to
have been no permanent post established for mere
trading purposes until the English régime. A military
fort erected during the early years of the eighteenth
century a few miles from its mouth,[45] furnished a
rendezvous for coureurs de bois and other traders, and,
unquestionably, considerable trade was carried on
because this region abounded in fur-bearing animals
and was easily accessible to posts on the shores of
Lake Michigan. Moreover, missionaries had invaded
the section as early as 1700,[46] and in those days of old,
priest and trader followed each other closely; where
one wrought, the other was sure to be found. No
doubt also the rise of trading posts in this valley was
retarded by Cadillac's policy of drawing the savages
to Detroit.

42. *Wis. Hist. Colls.*, XVIII, 99-100, 192; Wis. Hist. Society
    Proceedings, 1889, p. 73; Brymner, *Canadian Archives*,
    1905, I, 154.
43. Memoir of Bougainville, *Wis. Hist. Colls.*, XVIII, 192.
44. *Wis. Hist. Colls.*, XVIII, 101.
45. *Ibid*, XVI, 362.
46. *Mich. Hist. Colls.*, XXVIII, 181.

This was the region of trade for the Miamis and Potawatomi;[47] but Iroquois and English influence was strong, hence it was difficult to hold their allegiance without continually loading them with presents.[48] Charlevoix relates that in 1721 when he visited the post several Indians had just returned from British camps, whither they had gone with furs and from whence they brought back an abundant supply of liquor.[49]

Generally, the Governor General farmed out the forest commerce here to the commandants at the military post.[50] During the latter part of the forties, these farmers were permitted to stay there free of charge, though at other times a license had been required for this privilege.[51] In 1757 the commandant was paid a salary on condition that he support his post.[52] It has been estimated that about four hundred packs of lynxes, bears, cats, otters, stags, and deer were sent up annually.[53]

Little need be said of the fortunes of the separate posts during the last of the French and Indian wars. Trade was interfered with, and Englishmen were doing their best to incite the savages and withdraw their allegiance and trade from the French, while the latter were exerting their utmost efforts to keep them loyal.[54]

47. Wis. Hist. Colls., XVIII, 184-5.
48. Ibid, XVI, 394-5; 398-9.
49. Charlevoix, Journal of V. to N. A., II, 105.
50. Wis. Hist. Colls., XVII, 7, 445.
51. Ibid, 450-1.
52. Ibid, XVIII, 184-5.
53. Ibid.
54. Letter from La Jonquière to French Minister, Wis. Hist. Colls., XVIII, 67; Ibid, 80-81; Letter from Vaudreuil to

The French fur-trading régime in Michigan was nearing a close. That does not mean the disappearance of the French trader, for he remained within her territory for many years; but the official occupation of France ended and her old monopolistic fur-trade policy gave way for that of another people. The French régime saw the posts at Sault Ste. Marie, Michilimackinac, and Detroit, successively rise into prominence as important trading centers with minor posts dependent wholly or in part upon them, and French traders had invaded and established posts in the St. Joseph, Grand, and Kalamazoo river valleys. With the fall of Quebec in 1759, Michigan passed under English rule and the English trader began to enjoy part of the trade of his French predecessor.

54. Con. French Minister, *Ibid*, 156-7; *N. Y. Col. Docs.*, X, 401; Instructions for Vaudreuil from the king, *Wis. Hist. Colls.*, XVIII, 153-5.

CHAPTER IV

British Policy and Early Trade in Michigan

WHEN Great Britain extended her dominion over Michigan lands, she had already long realized the importance of the fur trade and done her best to get, if possible, a lion's share of the precious peltries.[1] Her policy was to encourage it, and to discourage all monopolies by making it equally free to all, that no one colony or people should wholly control it.[2] In 1763 King George III declared that all the trade with the Indians should be free and open to every one of his subjects, provided they secured a license from the governor or commander-in-chief of the colony where they resided, and promised to observe all trade regulations passed from time to time. These licenses were

1. Letter of Ramezay and Bégon to French Minister, *Wis. Hist. Colls.*, XVI, 331-3. Letter from Beauharnois and Hocquart to French Minister, *Ibid*, XVII, 75-6, 133; *Mich. Hist. Colls.*, XIX, 11, 12.
2. *N. Y. Col. Docs.*, VII, 572-81: *Mich. Hist. Colls.*, XXXVI, 43; Brymner *Canadian Archives*, 1906, 433.
   Thos. Gage in a letter March 20, 1762, says: "Immediately after we became masters of this country, all monopolies were abolished and all Incumbrances removed."—*Mich. Hist. Colls.*, XIX, 17. Lord Shelburne in 1767 suggests that the need of centralization of the management of Indian trade had passed with the withdrawal of the French from America. He advocates the abolishment of the office of superintendent and the placing of trade regulations in the control of the colonies. *N. Y. Col. Docs.*, VII, 981.

to be granted without fee, or reward, but might be declared void if the regulations were not observed.[3] One striking characteristic, then, of the British fur-trade régime is its freer policy. It will be seen later how this very freedom led to a scheming and under-selling in trade, a competition which brought on lawlessness and bitter feuds, until the wiser traders from sheer desperation sought to combine their interests to protect trade. Thus came into play the great fur-trading companies like that of the North West and the Mackinac; companies which gradually absorbed more and more of the Northwest commerce in peltries, scattering their fur-trading posts, agents, and clerks everywhere where were to be found the Indians and their hunting grounds. Companies and independent traders worked side by side in this régime, often, to be sure, coming into conflict.

A practice already used by the French,[4] which cost the British dear in both trouble and cash and which became a great item in securing trade, was the giving of presents to the Indians. By this means they aimed to entice them from other traders, no doubt expecting

---

3. King's Proclamation of 1763, *Mich. Hist. Colls.*, XXXVI, 14-19.

   Grignon, tells how about 1782 a certain Jean Marie Ducharme left Mackinac to trade without the required license from Gov. Sinclair, who for his disobedience demanded 1,500 bundles of wild hay for the king's public supply, or pay the penalty. About the same time Paul de la Croix departed on a trading voyage without permission. The same penalty was asked, but De la Croix said he did not think the king needed any hay, so he positively refused to furnish it. *Wis. Hist. Colls.*, III, 233.

4. The Jesuits' complaint at Michilimackinac that commandant and soldiers had introduced the practice of giving presents has been mentioned. See *Jes. Rel.*, LXV, 205, 203.

a present of furs in return. They taught him a bad habit, since thereafter, his trade and service had to be bought. Unscrupulous officers reaped a rich harvest from these presents and constant complaints were made asking that they be reduced. But the Indian expected them, so to keep his friendship and trade the practice had to be maintained.[5]

Gen. Thomas Gage, in a letter March 20, 1761, recommended that the smaller western posts be abandoned and that troops with proper officers be placed in the others, naming, among the five largest to be maintained, Michilimackinac and Detroit.[6] This policy was carried out. Posts established merely for purposes of trade were relinquished and strong garrisons placed in those remaining, that English authority might be respected by the coureurs de bois and the savages.[7] The red men were indeed reluctant to extend a hand of welcome to these reserved, practical-minded Britons, who came to take the place of their happy-go-lucky, ease-loving Frenchmen.

Such in brief was their policy of trade; a policy whose essential features stand in striking contrast with those of the preceding régime. France attempted to place this traffic in peltries in the hands of a few,

5. Mich. Hist. Colls., XIX, 173, 371, 517-18, 548, 658-661; Ibid., X, 393, 503-4, 514, 585; Ibid., XI, 320-21; XII, 146-7, 157-9; XVI, 653-6; XXIII, 604.
   Jan. 1, 1761, Capt. D. Campbell writes to Boquet: "The Indians expect Presents from us, I have done everything in my Power to keep them in temper; I have been obliged to issue them Provisions and small Presents." Mich. Hist. Colls., XIX, 70. An estimate of Indian presents for Detroit in 1782-3 is given in Ibid, XI, 382.
6. Ibid, XIX, 17-18.
7. Wis. Hist. Colls., VII, 151.

a fur-trading aristocracy, and piled decree upon decree to hold it there, control it, limit it, and preserve it; the result was, illegal trade on every hand and defiance of the laws and decrees which men considered unjust. England made it free to all for the mere asking; a policy which ended in disaster, because men unwilling to control their greed for the precious pelts waged bitter war with one another, each bent on obtaining the biggest share. The former usually treated the savage with kindness and won his affection by making him an equal,—living, mingling, and intermarrying with him. Though he gave fewer presents, at times less brandy and lower prices for his furs, yet he held him loyal. The latter did not bear in mind that this child of the forest never forgot a kindness nor forgave a wrong, but treated him as an inferior that could be bought with presents; hence severity and harshness characterized his attitude toward the Indian and he trampled on the red man's rights until the latter rose in rebellion, which ended in Pontiac's conspiracy and war. The former had established many posts as entrepots of trade, and had smaller outposts and temporary rendezvous scattered in many places; the latter sought to abandon all useless posts, aiming to strengthen and fortify the larger and more lucrative.

Such were some of the differences in their policy of trade. Many similarities might be pointed out, such as the old system of giving credits, and the efforts made to preserve the hunting grounds against incoming settlers. But these concern us less here. The British régime of trade in Michigan must now be considered; first the pre-Revolutionary period, when English traders slowly succeeded to French influence in trade;

secondly, its progress while American colonies were struggling for independence. The first of these periods is the subject of this chapter.

At the close of the French and Indian War, Major Robert Rogers was ordered by General Amherst to take charge of the western posts and arrived at Detroit November 29, 1761, without opposition in raising the British colors.[8] The winter of 1761 passed quietly. With the exception of a few officers and their families most of the residents remained. The Indians went out to hunt, and the monotony was only broken now and then by the coming and going of traders seeking licenses to trade and conferences held with the Indians. Besides the soldiers, about forty fur traders and engagés are said to have been stationed here.[9]

Michilimackinac until 1761 remained in possession of the French, who continued to pursue their commerce in peltries, until George Etherington, the first English commandant, arrived. He summoned the inhabitants of the surrounding region to meet him and swear allegiance to the new government. Many, no doubt, made this an occasion for bringing their furs to market.[10]

For a Briton to venture single-handed among hostile Indians and into the midst of unfriendly French, but recently conquered, must have called for more than ordinary courage and pluck, yet that is just what Alexander Henry, the first authorized English trader

8. Croghan's Journal, *Western Travels*, I, 100-125; *Wis. Hist. Colls.*, XVIII, 223-229. *Mich. Hist. Colls.*, XIX, 40-42.
9. *Wis. Hist. Colls.*, XVIII, 228; *Mich. Hist. Colls.*, XIX, 121; Parkman, *Conspiracy of Pontiac*, 190.
10. *Wis. Hist. Colls.*, VII, 151-2; *Ibid*, III, 223. Among those mentioned as responding to the call of Etherington are Augustin and Chas. Langlade.

at Michilimackinac did.   Having obtained permission from Gen. Thomas Gage to go to Michilimackinac to trade, he secured goods at Albany.   Adopting the costume of a voyageur and placing himself under the guidance of an old French trader, Etienne Campion, he left for that place in the middle of August.[11]   About thirty families who depended for their living upon the Indian traders going to and coming from Montreal[12] were then living there.

His disguise did not conceal him, as he had not been long at Michilimackinac when he was informed that a band of Chippewa Indians were coming from the island to see him.   Farley, an interpreter in French employ, told him it was the custom for the Indians to visit a strange trader and bring a small present in expectation of securing a large one in return, but as Henry was an Englishman, it was difficult to tell just what they would do.   About sixty warriors arrived and their chief proceeded to deliver a speech in which he said that the French king was their father upon whom the English had made war, therefore robbed him of his land, while he, old and infirm that he was, had been taking a nap; the French perhaps were conquered but the savage was not, he had yet to be reckoned with; the English had killed many a red man in the late war and savage blood thirsted for revenge for it was Indian custom to retaliate; but there was another way out of the difficulty, presents could do wonders; so far, however, the English king had presented them with no gifts nor tried to come

11. *Minn. Hist. Colls.*, III, 339. Masson, *Les Bourgeois*, I, 10-11; Henry, *Travels and Adventures*, 10-12.
12. Henry, *Travels and Adventures*, 40.

to any agreement with them in the shape of a treaty; they could adopt no new father until that was done; their father and friend was the French king. "But for you," said the chief, "we have taken into consideration, that you have ventured your life among us, in the expectation that we should not molest you. You do not come armed, with an intention of making war; you come in peace, to trade with us, and supply us with the necessaries, of which we are in much want. We shall regard you, therefore, as a brother; and you may sleep tranquilly, without fear of the Chippewas."[13] Henry responded by granting them a few presents and telling them that France had given Canada to the English and that henceforth the English king was their father.[14]

Having thus made his peace with the Chippewas, he hoped to live and trade in peace, together with two other traders, Stanley Goddard, and Ezekiel Solomons, who had arrived from Montreal.[15] But there were other visitors, less friendly, ready to call. Two hundred Ottawas arrived from L'Arbre Croche and demanded that the English traders give to each of their young men merchandise and ammunition to the amount of fifty beaver skins on credit. This would have stripped them of all they had, so they refused. But the Indians were not to be denied; they gave them a day to consider the matter, threatening that unless the traders yielded, their goods would be taken from them; for they were forfeited goods, the English having made no treaty with the Indians.

13. *Ibid*, 41-45. This was the speech of Minavavana.
14. *Ibid*, 46.
15. *Ibid*, 48.

Farley advised Henry and his friends to yield, saying that unless they did, the Indians might kill them, but the British traders suspecting Farley's sincerity, thinking he was simply preying upon their fear to induce them to abandon the Indian trade, prepared to resist. Fortunately, in the morning three hundred troops of the sixth regiment under command of Lieutenant Leslie marched into the fort and the traders were safe.[16]

They were saved, it is true, but by a mere chance. Moreover, as long as they remained and surely if they attempted to penetrate farther into this region, they were in danger of losing their lives. It took a stout heart to continue to live in such a hostile atmosphere, so it is little wonder that old French posts and regions of trade like Sault Ste. Marie and the St. Joseph Valley were not quickly peopled with British dealers in pelts.

The former could scarcely be spoken of as a particularly flourishing post at this time. In 1762, Henry tells us, there were only four houses, that of the governor, that of the interpreter, and two others used as barracks. The only family living there was M. Cadotte, the interpreter, and his wife a Chippewa woman. The commandant managed the Indian trade on government account. There was a village of about fifty-five Chippewas, but the majority of these went westward to hunt in the summer.[17] Some trade must have been carried on also on the River St. Joseph, as J. D. Hambach speaks of going there in 1762, his goods having been sent before him.[18]

16. *Ibid.*, 47-51. *Mich. Hist. Colls.*, XIX, 116.
17. Henry, *Travels and Adventures*, 58.
18. Bouquet Papers, *Mich. Hist. Colls.*, XIX, 156.

But the British trader hesitated to follow immediately in the footsteps of the French. "There were plenty of diligent traders among the English," says Wilson, "but they shrank from penetrating into the wilderness, for they fully realized the Indians' hostility toward them." "Patiently", says he, "they waited for the French trader. Spring came and found them at the deserted posts with their canoes and sledges loaded with furs, but no Frenchman appeared."[19] The coureurs de bois, that reckless, light-hearted forest tramp, as well as licensed trader, looked askance at these more sober, exacting Englishmen and found it difficult to become accustomed to their ways; so that it was not until after Pontiac's War in 1765-6, when the Indians had been thoroughly subdued and the British felt themselves[20] masters, that trade really began in earnest. From then it continued to flourish until the Revolutionary War, when it was once more hampered, though not stopped.

Yet considerable trade must have been carried on in Michigan before that time, as in 1761 H. T. Cramahe sent to Gov. Murray the following estimate of goods consumed in Indian trade at various posts; presumably in 1760, though he does not say so. The value of merchandise sold at Detroit, exclusive of Illinois commerce, according to Montreal prices was 350,000 livres; at Michilimackinac, exclusive of Illinois commerce, 250,000 livres, and at St. Joseph, 60,000 livres.[21] Thomas Gage reports a list of posts in the upper country where Indian trade was pursued in

19. Willson, *The Great Company*, II, 25-28.
20. Masson, *Les Bourgeois*, I, 9.
21. *Mich. Hist. Colls.*, XIX, 14.

1762, and among them are noted the following: among posts sold to particular persons are Sault Ste. Marie, sold at 14,000 livres, and St. Joseph at 3,000. Among the free posts are named Michilimackinac and Detroit. Passes for canoes to these posts were paid at the rate of 600 livres and they were obliged to carry 400 weight for the king.[22]

That a great deal of this trade was by Frenchmen is certain, for the British foothold in Michigan was far from secure. The insolence of these haughty new-comers and their ill treatment of the Indian was not likely to inspire him with friendship, but rather to arouse his rebellious and savage nature.[23] Pontiac plotted revenge. All English posts were to be razed to the ground, and all Englishmen killed.[24] Michigan posts and Michigan trade were doomed to suffer and come to a stand-still, at least for a time. Sault Ste. Marie had been abandoned the previous year, hence escaped the awful fate of St. Joseph and Michilimackinac.[25] The story of the massacres at the latter posts have often been told and need not be repeated here. Suffice it to say, the English traders did not escape. A canoe-load of these arriving from Montreal while Michilimackinac was being attacked, were seized, dragged through the water, beaten and imprisoned. Of the English traders Mr. Tracy alone lost his life; Ezekiel Solomons and Mr. Bostwick were taken by the Ottawas and later carried to Montreal for ransom.

22. *Ibid*, 21.
23. *N. Y. Col. Docs.*, VII, 689, 836, 929, 955, 960, 964, 987.
24. According to Gorrel's Journal, Pontiac's War was fostered and encouraged by French traders. *Wis. Hist. Colls.*, I, 26, see also *N. Y. Col. Docs.*, VII, 929.
25. Parkman, *Conspiracy of Pontiac*, 317.

Alexander Henry was saved through the kindness of a friend.[26] Detroit fought desperately to hold its own, and finally succeeded in warding off the Indian attack and saving the fort.[27]

After the massacre, Michilimackinac was practically abandoned for a year. Henry tells that on visiting the place in 1764 he found only two French traders and a few Indians.[28] That same year, Captain Howard re-established the post, bringing there a garrison,[29] and the following year Alexander Henry applied for and was granted by the commander-in-chief at Michilimackinac the exclusive trade of the Lake Superior region. He was to have four canoes on twelve months' credit which were to be paid for in beaver pelts.[30] He evidently pushed trade to the utmost, for he is said to have obtained in three days while on a short expedition to the north shore, twelve thousand beaver skins besides many martens and other furs.[31] But he was not the only one pushing trade, for the field was now open. British traders could enter with less fear for their lives, and many made use of the opportunity to make this splendid trading mart their place of abode.

While Michilimackinac was slowly assuming its former position in the fur-trading world, at Detroit, too, trading relations with the Indians were resumed. Croghan tells how, in October 1765, several Indian

26. Henry, *Travels and Adventures*, 105-6.
27. *Ibid*, 185.
28. Henry, *Travels and Adventures*, 155.
29. *Wis. Hist. Colls.*, XVIII, 270.
30. *Minn. Hist. Colls.*, III, 339; Masson, *Les Bourgeois*, I, 10-11; Henry, *Travels and Adventures*, 192-96.
31. *Minn. Hist. Colls.*, III, 339.

nations informed Colonel Campbell and himself that they wished their new fathers, the English, would re-open trade with them that fall; at least, send some traders to winter among them, otherwise they would have to go to the French. The chiefs of some of the bands of the Ottawas, Hurons, Chippewas, and Potowatomi came to Detroit; some expressing their satisfaction that peace with the Indians had been re-established, others soliciting trade. The Ottawa, Potowatomi, and Chippewa chiefs declared that they were willing to allot to the English land necessary for trading purposes, provided they were paid for it.[32]

So trade began to flourish once more, and for some time the peltry dealers were the dominant force in this little post. They were not as a class over-scrupulous as to what they did, but strained every nerve to get as many peltries as possible. Complaints came to General Haldimand that in spite of all pre-cautions, fur traders would land their batteaux in the outskirts of the woods about three miles from Detroit, make bargains with and cheat the Indians. They lodged the peltry secured in an old French house, leaving it there until opportunity to bring it to the post presented itself. These rude, uncouth frontiers-men had matters much their own way, according to Major Henry Bassett, who calls them "the outcasts of all nations, the refuse of mankind;" he claimed that all articles even to a few eggs had to be purchased from them, and that while they had the market cornered they made good use of it, charging exorbitant prices.[33]

32. Croghan's Journal, *Western Travels*, I, 159-161; *Hist. of Ionia and Montcalm Cos.*, 18.
33. Haldimand Papers, *Mich. Hist. Colls.*, XIX, 297-8; *Ibid*, XX, 288.

Meanwhile, J. B. Cadotte established a trading house at Sault Ste. Marie about 1765,[34] and Alexander Henry who visited the place in 1767 reports that provisions were extremely low, as the fishery had failed that year.[35] John Long tells of stopping there in 1768 and finding a small fort built by Indians, and about ten log houses for the residence of English and French traders; but he does not state whether these were occupied.[36]

Slowly yet surely the English trader was beginning to gain a firm foothold. Search for peltries, as in the previous régime, was the great business of the day; a business in which the "almighty dollar" was the beaver pelt, which could purchase all the Indian's and white man's necessaries, and could itself be bought from the savage for a mere pint of rum; a business favored not only by the actual participants but by British officials as well, judging from the report of the Lord Commissioners for Trade and Plantations, in which they say: "It does appear to us that the extension of the fur trade depends entirely upon the Indians being undisturbed in possession of their hunting ground, and that all colonizating does in its nature, and must in its consequences, operate to the prejudice of that branch of commerce... Let the savages enjoy their deserts in quiet. Were they driven from their forests their peltry-trade would decrease."[37] Sentiments like these show somewhat the English estimation of the value of the fur trade.[38]

34. Masson, *Les Bourgeois*, I, 11.
35. Henry, *Travels and Adventures*, 206-7.
36. Long's Voyages, *Western Travels*, II, 79.
37. Winsor, *Nar. and Crit. Hist.*, VI, 687-8. Sparks, *Benj. Franklin*, IV, 313-14.
38. See also Hansard, *Parliamentary Debates*, XXIII, 382, 409.

This early period of the British fur-trade régime, the pre-Revolutionary, was transitional, a passing from French policy and influence to that of the English; a period in which they gained a firm hold on Michigan trade, subdued the Indian, and to a certain extent enlisted him on their side against a coming enemy, the American. They were soon to face two struggles; one a bitter feud among the many individual traders, each trying to enrich himself in this forest commerce at the expense of his neighbor,—a feud which culminated in the organization of trading companies; another, the Revolutionary War, which culminated in independence for the Colonies and snatched from Great Britain her western hunting grounds. The operation, influence, and effect of these two contests on the Michigan fur trade will next be considered.

CHAPTER V

MICHIGAN FUR TRADE IN REVOLUTIONARY TIMES

NATURALLY it would seem that a time of war with its manifold problems would be far from conducive to the fur trade, and that therefore this commerce in the Revolutionary era would hold little of interest; but the main scene of the contest between loyalist and patriot lay in other regions; though it hampered, yet it did not stop this trade in Michigan, because the Indians on many of the hunting grounds whence came her peltries remained practically undisturbed. Three phases of the period must be taken into account. To be sure, the effect of war has its place; but of far greater concern here is that contest waged between individual traders in almost every little trading mart on the frontier; a war keen, bitter, deadly, and of considerable moment in the trading world, for out of it grew the great fur-trading companies. Then, too, of utmost importance, though not confined strictly to the Revolutionary period, in the English régime we see the creeping in of American influence through the entrance of the Yankee trader who sought here a new field for his operations.

The war made itself felt. It caused unrest among the Indians and thus endangered the life of the traders. Numerous rumors reached the posts of men who had been killed by the savages while on their way to the

hunting grounds.[1] Doubtless some of these murders
were the natural outcome of a general unrest that any
war would have caused; others were merited, as there
were traders who considered the savage outside the
pale of humane treatment and dealt with him accordingly. American influence too had crept in, and some
of these forest warriors favored[2] and fought for the
American cause; though on the whole it may be said
that, just as in the previous régime they remained
loyal to the French and fought against the English,
so now they joined the latter against the Yankee, the
new stranger who sought to invade their hunting
grounds.[3] But whatever the cause, these murders
spread alarm, and traders hesitated to penetrate into
the wilderness. Major Henry Basset of Detroit in
1773 denied passes for St. Joseph's Valley to English
and French alike, and informed the red men that
until they behaved better and ceased their depredations, no traders would be sent among them;[4] no mean
threat, as regarded by the Indian, for the white man
had many things he coveted and for which he had
cultivated a taste.

According to Gov. J. G. Simcoe, the fur trade at
Detroit suffered considerably during the war, because
certain Indian tribes on the Wabash from whence
that post usually obtained many peltries, withdrew
their allegiance and brought the produce of their hunt
to the Americans. "It is understood," said he after

1. *Mich. Hist. Colls.*, XIX, 301, 303, 304, 306. *Wis. Hist.
     Colls.*, XVIII, 310-11, 312-13, 342; *N. Y. Col. Docs.*, VII,
     929.
2. *Mich. Hist. Colls.*, XXV, 28-29.
3. *Wis. Hist. Colls.*, XI, 98-9, 100-11, 115-17, 119, 121-2.
4. *Mich. Hist. Colls.*, XIX, 301.

the war, "that these nations have now returned to
their former places of residence, and that commerce
will revert to its former course, unless the armies of
the United States take post on the Miamis River, the
channel by which a most considerable part of peltries
are conveyed to Detroit."[5]

When the war closed the Indians were in a turmoil.
"They are fierce and warlike," declared Montreal
merchants in a memorial, "and unfortunately for the
traders are in cruel war with each other."[6]   At Michilimackinac they were almost beyond control.[6] John
Dease who had been made deputy superintendent of
the Indians in 1786, removed to that place from
Niagara.   After holding several councils with representatives from the various Indian tribes, he finally
concluded a treaty of peace with them in July, 1787,
in which they acknowledged the king of England as
their father, next to the Great Spirit, and promised
henceforth to deal honestly with the white traders
even to giving them their share of justice if they
deserve it.[7]

To adjust successfully relations with the Indian
during this period was no mean undertaking, but
rather one taxing Englishmen's ingenuity to the
utmost. Not only must they gain and hold the
affection of that fickle being, but they must maintain
friendly relations between the various tribes.   Without
the former their own traders were liable to be attacked
and killed, while the trade was usurped by the Yankees;
and without the latter, profit from trade would be
slim for both Yankee and Briton.

5. *Ibid*, XXV, 28-9.
6. *Ibid*, XI, 483-4, 485.
7. *Ibid*, XI, 490-6; 499-501; XXIII, 606-7.

Yet another problem confronted the Michigan dealer in pelts; it was not the getting of furs but how to transport them and secure merchandise for exchange, as intercourse with the Eastern markets was cut off again and again.[8]

What were the means of transportation in those days? Largely the birch-bark canoes and private trading vessels. The former, which continued to ply our lakes far into the nineteenth century in the interest of trade, were little crafts which could hold from two to fourteen paddlers. When carrying merchandise they were usually manned by three men and held a cargo of twenty hundred weight; yet so light were they that a person might carry one on his back over the portages.[9] Ninety to a hundred of these, Charles Grant tells us in 1780, went up annually to Michilimackinac on Lakes Huron and Michigan to La Baye and the Northwest, and he claimed that more would be needed now, as they would have to carry all provisions formerly coming from Detroit.[10]

In the days of the Northwesters, the annual trips of their trading canoes, twenty, thirty, fifty, nay more in number, to Michilimackinac and Sault Ste. Marie were interesting events in the early trade; to the few dwellers at the Sault, the greatest events in the year; the arrival of those jolly voyageurs of old with their canoes laden with merchandise was looked forward

8.   Askin's letter-book, 7, 15, 127-8; Brymner, *Canadian Archives*,
        1890, 58. See *Mich. Hist. Colls.*, XI, 424, for a petition
        from Detroit merchants, asking for the privilege of using
        private vessels to carry their peltries to Montreal.
9.   La Hontan, *N. V. to N. A.*, I, 62-5; Mackenzie, *Voyages*,
        I, xxvii-xxx.
10.   *Mich. Hist. Colls.*, XIX, 509.

to for days.   When they reached the Sault the freight
was unpacked, boats were poled near the shore and
after a day, perhaps two or three, of continual feasting
and revel, these men, athletic and hard as nails because
of the life they led, again loaded their boats and
proceeded on their journey to the Grand Portage and
other points.[11]

So much for the canoe.   La Salle's "Griffin," lost
at sea, was the forerunner of the private trading
vessel on the Great Lakes.   As the fur trade increased
and was pursued on a larger scale, men began to build
vessels to carry their goods, vessels of from ninety to
one hundred tons.[12]   In 1774 Samuel Robertson came
to Detroit, sent by the London firm of Phyn and
Ellice to command a small craft for some merchants
trading at Michilimackinac.   Later, he owned two
small vessels in partnership with John Askin and Jean
Baptiste Barthe, which sailed on Lakes Huron and
Michigan.[13]   Gen. Haldimand, in 1784, granted permission to the North West Company to build a small
vessel at Detroit for the Lake Superior trade.[14]   The
"Nancy," in the service of the XY company,[15] the
"Speedwell," the "Iroquois;"[16] the "General Hunter,"
the "Beaver," the "Athabasca"[17] were busy transporting peltries and bringing goods for exchange during
the English régime.

11.   Wis. Hist. Society *Proceedings*, 1889, 77-82; Fowle, "Old
        Times at the Sault," Sault *Evening News*, Feb. 22, 1913.
12.   Mackenzie, *Voyages*, xxxviii.
13.   *Wis. Hist. Colls.*, XIX, 241n.
14.   Brymner, *Canadian Archives*, 1888, 72; *Ibid*, 1890, 61.
15.   *Wis. Hist. Colls.*, XIX, 308,—refers to Ontario Hist. Soc.
        Papers, VI, 22, 27-32.
16.   Burnett's ledger, blotter, and day-book.
17.   Askin's blotter and petty ledgers.

But when war began, orders were issued that only the king's vessels, carrying provisions should be allowed passage.[18] This was a hard blow to the fur trade, for even the trading crafts going from Detroit to Michilimackinac were stopped.[19] Capt. Bannerman, coming from the former place with rum and corn for the Northwest trade, was forced to take oath that no part was for any other use.[20] John Askin, who was engaged in Indian trade during this period, complained again and again of the lack of provisions.[21] He relates how a vessel coming from Detroit was loaded with provisions for several, where his goods alone would have filled her twice over.[22]

Askin was at this time busy forwarding supplies for the traders of the Northwest and on him depended men like the Messrs. McGill, the Frobishers, Patterson, Alexander Henry, Todd and McGill, Holmes and Grant, Richard Dobie, and others who had trading interests at Grand Portage and elsewhere in the Northwest, for their supplies of corn, grease or tallow, flour, sugar, and above all liquor.[23] Not to disappoint them in times like these, when transportation was so often stopped, was quite a problem and he was often at his wits' end to furnish what they demanded. Lake Superior shores, Detroit, and Milwaukee were canvassed for the needed corn, grease, and flour, but the brandy had to be brought from Eastern markets.[24]

18. Askin's letter-book, 49-50. *Mich. Hist. Colls.*, XI, 424, 448.
19. *Wis. Hist. Colls.*, XIX, 236-7, 239; Brymner, *Canadian Archives*, 1888, 61.
20. Askin's letter-book, 49-50, 61.
21. See references in note 8.
22. *Wis. Hist. Colls.*, XIX, 236.
23. Askin's letter-book, 1-49ff.
24. *Ibid.*

On June 6, 1778, he wrote Benjamin Frobisher that he had, that spring, only five barrels of spirits sent up; had not been able to keep even two for his own use; and not a pound of flour had been sent him that season, because Lieutenant Governor Hamilton commanded that only thirteen thousand weight was to leave Detroit, and that was only to be granted to persons right on the spot, or to those who had others there to swear it was for trading purposes.[25] In a letter of July he complained that his vessel instead of being permitted to carry his own provisions was forced to carry those of the king.[26]

Neither traders nor traders' supplies were allowed to go into the upper country without a pass from military authorities;[27] yet the British Government aimed to have men on the hunting grounds, to barter with the savage and keep him in good humor. Major De Peyster, writing from Michilimackinac in 1779, told Governor Haldimand that it was absolutely necessary to send up canoes with goods so that friendly Indians might have traders among them. He asked for twenty of these, said that number would be sufficient, as with fewer canoes better care could be taken in distributing them; then, too, they could better prevent them from falling into the enemies' hands. Out of these, twenty-two were to be sent to Mr. Barthe at Sault Ste. Marie, and one to Mr. Cadott.[28]

The difficulty of securing supplies and sending peltries to market presented itself in intenser form

25. *Ibid*, 48-50.
26. *Ibid*, 164-5.
27. *Wis. Hist. Colls.*, XI, 135n, 133-4.
28. *Ibid*, 133-4.

at Detroit than at Michilimackinac; for the former
post lay nearer the scene of war, and traffic by the
lower route was more easily shut off than by the upper.
So merchants were in a sorry plight to secure goods
for the Indian trade and forward them to posts like
Sault Ste. Marie and Michilimackinac, as the king's
vessels proved inadequate in supplying their needs.[29]

In fact, they held that unless means of transportation
were furnished, all trade at the latter post would stop.
One year, said they, owing to the late arrival of merchandise, over one thousand packs of fur, which usually were brought to Detroit, had been sent to New Or-
leans, and many traders who came to the post for supplies were turned away. Hence in 1785 they petitioned
Governor Hamilton that they be permitted to use
the "Gage," a vessel which at the time was in their
harbor; for if the existing condition of affairs continued,
their trade would be ruined. Without goods they
could not trade, and to get goods was not an easy
task.[30]   This hindrance to transportation proved,
indeed, one of the chief obstacles that the Revolutionary War placed in the way of the Michigan fur trade.

But, while this war for American independence
was in progress, stopping transportation and hindering
the forest commerce, another conflict was waged
within many a frontier trading post.   England's liberal
policy of trade and the success of her pioneer traders
led many unscrupulous adventurers to embark in
this enterprise; men of all classes and conditions who
cared little for law, justice, and a square deal, so long

29. *Askin Papers*, I, 167; *Mich. Hist. Colls.*, XI, 458-60.
30. *Mich. Hist. Colls.*, XI, 4598-; see also Brymner, *Canadian
     Archives*, 1890, 59-60, 57-58, for petitions from men
     interested in the affairs of the North West Company.

as the main purpose of their undertaking prospered; men who had little respect for the rights of each other, much less for those of the savage.[31] But the latter had to be considered, for as a rule, he alone furnished the coveted beaver pelt. To get this from him, resort was had to any means that proved serviceable; and one of the most effective was to furnish him liberal quantities of liquor.

To be sure, this was contrary to the decrees of the government. As early as 1762 they had made an attempt to stop this traffic.[32] In 1777 an ordinance was passed against it, but English merchants clamored for its repeal. To refuse the Indian rum, said they, meant ruin to trade;[33] so, like the coureurs de bois of the French régime, they paid no attention to ordinances and decrees and smuggled it in, whenever they pleased. A story related by Thomas Bentley of a liquor deal at Michilimackinac, shows one way in which the law was evaded; although orders had been repeatedly issued against furnishing liquor to the savages, yet the Indians were continually drunk. On inquiry among the Indians, he found that a certain Mr. De Rocheblave traded it to them in the night for beaver and other skins. He had the Indians trained not to come to him by day nor to expose his illegal traffic. He even went so far as to place in chains two of them who had dared to report him.[34] Thus traders steeped the savage in brandy when opportunity offered, that he might be more willing

31. Masson, *Les Bourgeois*, I, 17-19; *Western Travels*, II, 15-16.
32. *Mich. Hist. Colls.*, XIX, 128, 148.
33. *Ibid*, XXIV, 111-12.
34. *Ibid*, XIX, 330.

to part with his furs and more easily cheated. No doubt, he who could furnish the biggest share of drinks, got the biggest share of peltries.[35]

This was one way of getting the skins of the red man; another was to undersell and overbid rivals in trade. Hence ensued a competition, fierce, merciless, unlicensed, ruinous, for this was the régime of the free trader and independent merchant, who acted for self, and self alone, exploiting natives and fellow traders alike for the largest immediate gain. This merciless rivalry engendered a feeling of hostility so bitter that quarrels, fights, and murders became common. To clear the field of the other fellow and get his trade was the all-absorbing question in this heartless régime, and to many it mattered not what means were used; where they could not drive them away, they could at least send them to happier hunting grounds. Here was genuine war of a most hideous sort waged in the frontier posts, all for a mere beaver pelt.[36] Mackinac was naturally a favorite resort for such traders, and, consequently, became the focus of a bitter competition fatal to all profit. Here were the Henry's, the Pond's, the McDonald's, the Cameron's, the Aird's, the Howard's, the Morrison's, the Lyon's, the Solomon's, and the McBeath's, all representatives of Montreal firms, each anxious to advance the interests of his own concern. Here were government employees who could not resist the temptation of turning trader when opportunity presented itself. Here were men like John Askin who made this a central location for

35. The Indians were so anxious to secure liquor that they even
     killed traders who refused to give it to them. *Ibid*, XIX,
     296.
36. Masson, *Les Bourgeois*, I, 17-19; *Western Travels*, II, 15-16.

outstanding interests. Here were numerous independent traders, eager for gain, to be obtained by
fair means or foul.[37]

It soon became evident that for each to pursue his
own interest, with no concern or regard for others, was
disastrous to all; so in 1779, Ezekiel Solomons and
others petitioned Major De Peyster, their commandant,
for permission to establish a general store in which
all traders might place their goods and pool the receipts.
This was granted.[38] The association formed was to
last a year and all members were to put their merchandise together for trading purposes, each securing a
share of the proceeds in proportion to his stock. All
subscribers promised, under penalty of losing their
goods, to abandon private trade with the Indians
or with any other person whose trade would injure
the company. Persons qualified for dealing with the
Indians were to be chosen by the general vote of the
subscribers. If the choice was approved by the
commandant, these were obliged to go where he
permitted the members of the company to send them.
Those outside of the Association were allowed six
days for considering whether they were willing to
join; if by that time they had decided to the contrary,
they were forever excluded. Every member who had
men employed during the winter should be obliged
to admit them to the society, when the committee
found them capable; and all persons who had given
credit to the Indians before the agreement were at

37. *Wis. Hist. Colls.*, XIX, 236, 238, 249, 254; see the signa-
       tures of the Association of the General Store at Michili-
       mackinac, *Mich. Hist. Colls.*, X, 307.
38. *Mich. Hist. Colls.*, X, 305, 367, 499, 600: Brymner, *Canadian
       Archives*, 1888, 61.

liberty to collect it, provided they had notified the committee chosen to take charge of the company's affairs.[39]

Their interests on the River St. Joseph were placed in the hands of Louis Chevalier and P. Hurtibise, who were forbidden to carry on any trade on their own account.[40]   Lyons, Bostick, Campion, and Reilhe, each sent goods to this place amounting to eight thousand livres; but the enterprise proved a failure and they sustained considerable losses, claiming that at the close of the year, goods to the value of thirty thousand livres as well as all profits of the season were taken by a band of robbers.[41]   Evidently they were not much more successful at Michilimackinac, for when the terms of agreement expired, in 1780, the company dissolved.   So traders were once more at liberty to pursue their competitive policy, and contention and feud became again the order of the day.

There seems to have been another effort at union among Michilimackinac traders, which ended in failure. This association, mentioned by Perrault, may have been the beginning of the Mackinaw Company, whose

---

39. *Mich. Hist. Colls.*, X, 305-7.   These articles were drawn up July 1, 1779, and were signed by the following: Robert Ord, Et. Campion, L. Ducharme, W. Gasse, J. B. Guillon, David McCrae & Co., Ezekiel Solomons, Henry Bostwick, Augt. Chabilley, A. Dubuc, B. Tabeau, Louis Chevallier, John Macnamara, A. Campion, Gamelin X (his mark), G. Cahn & Co., Benj. Lyon, J. Sanguinet, William Grant, M. Auge, Matthew Lessey, J. G. Zanelius, P. Chaboillez, Theodore & Grahame, James Bird.   The committee appointed to have charge of the companies' affairs were: "John Askin, Joseph Louis Ainé David Rinkin, Matthew Laissé, Augt. Chaboyer, & Mocrai."

40. *Mich. Hist. Colls.*, X, 600.

41. *Ibid*, 367.

origin is somewhat obscure.[42] He states that several outfitters of Montreal, who furnished goods for trade at this post, having come there, united for three years under the name of "General Company of Lake Superior and the South," and decided to equip and send men into the interior for trade. Perrault was one of these, who was engaged to winter with La Framboise on the Chippewa River. The first year did not prove prosperous. Then one of the chief directors died, business was poorly managed, several of the traders became bankrupt, and finally in 1787 the company dissolved.

Though these two efforts at united action in the trading world had proved a failure, two companies did arise that assumed permanent form and came to wield an enormous influence in trade. These were the North West and the Mackinaw companies, organized distinctly for trading purposes; a combination of merchants for the betterment and the protection of trade.

The North West Company, founded by 1783, was fully organized in 1787. When this organization first launched into the field of fur trade, the association was more or less in the nature of an experiment. Men like Benjamin Frobisher, Charles Patterson, William Holmes, Charles J. Baptiste, and others who had hitherto traded independently and found it so unsatisfactory, decided to join their forces and work in harmony. So in their first agreement it was stipulated that no money was to be paid into a common stock but that each partner was to furnish his proportion of goods necessary to carry on the trade.[43]

42. *Mich. Hist. Colls.*, XXXVII, 536-7, 539, 545.
43. Masson, *Les Bourgeois*, II, 459-60.

But it was felt that a closer and more permanent organization was needed, hence the old agreement was dissolved and a new partnership formed. Shareholders appointed from their number special agents, to import from England such goods as might be required and store them in Montreal. Their plan for. conducting trade was similar to that of the French. European goods, such articles as were desired by the Indians and traders, were packed and forwarded, and the money for outfits was supplied. Store houses were erected in convenient places on the borders of the lakes. Posts formerly· used by the French were occupied, and agents were sent to the great trading centers of the Northwest, among which were Michilimackinac, Sault Ste. Marie, and Detroit.[44] In these places furs were deposited when brought from the interior, packed, and sent to Montreal for shipment to England. Two vessels sailed the lakes in the interest of their trade. Later this company split, and a rival company arose known as the XY company.[45]

What became known as the Mackinaw Company was established about 1783-4. It is supposed to have been composed of some of the same mercantile firms as composed the North West Company. It operated largely through American territory, having its principal station at Mackinaw from whence it drew its name.[46]

Of these two companies, the latter got the firmer

44. Grand Portage was another great trade emporium, to which they sent their agents.
45. Mackenzie, *Voyages*, I, xvii-xxxix; Masson, *Les Bourgeois*, 459-99; *Minn. Hist. Colls.*, III, 340-41; Irving, *Astoria* (1806), I, 20-25; Wis. Hist. Society, *Proceedings*, 1889, 76-81; *Wis. Hist. Colls.*, XIX, 163-4.
46. *Wis. Hist. Colls.*, XVIII, 439-40n.

hold on Michigan trade, which was quite natural, because its central depot was located within her territory. Not only did this company usurp a large share of her forest commerce, but also a goodly portion of that of the Lake Superior and Mississippi regions as well. In fact, it became such a powerful rival of the Astor company which arose later, that Mr. Astor, rather than compete with it, sought to obtain a share in its stock, thus neutralizing the competition which would otherwise have arisen.[47]

To be sure, the North West Company was not without its stations of trade in Michigan; but its main depot for the western commerce was at Grand Portage, hence naturally it drew a large portion of its supplies from the region farther to the west and northwest.[48]

Hitherto, a competitive war had been waged between trader and trader; a war bitter and unceasing, because the opponents were, as a rule, about equally matched. The advent of companies did not put an end to this contest, it simply changed the contestants. It now meant a struggle between an individual and a powerful business concern; a struggle in which the small trader had little chance, and was often swept from the field or forced to combine his interests with those of a larger concern. However, many independent traders continued their operations in these western regions, and were able to hold their own against their more powerful rivals.

A Michigan trader who did not ally himself with any company was John Askin, whose extensive opera-

47. Chittenden, *Fur Trade of the Far West*, I, 309-10.
48. See reference in note 45.

tions at Michilimackinac during the Revolutionary War have already been noted.   While there he maintained an establishment with Jean Baptiste Barthe and Samuel Robertson at Sault Ste. Marie under the direction of a Mr. McDonnell, who served as clerk and forwarding agent.[49]   Later he removed to Detroit. Many of the firms and the men who had sought his supplies, while war was in progress, were now members of one of the two trading companies, and had withdrawn their patronage and trade.   It is highly probable, too, that he did not wish to cope with a concern like the Mackinaw Company, which was steadily increasing in strength and influence; and, perhaps, like Cadillac, looking for other fields to conquer, he saw in the southern trading mart new opportunities.   Be that as it may, he left Michilimackinac and became a prominent dealer in pelts at Detroit.   Interesting are the ledgers and blotters he kept while there, and they throw considerable light on the fur trade at this post in the nineties.   That the Detroit commerce in pelts was not confined to its immediate neighborhood, but that many traders from distant sections sought this depot, depositing their furs and getting merchandise in return is evident.   Hither William Anderson, and François La Fontaine brought their peltries from the Miamis, Laurant Bazadonne from Vincennes, Jean Langlois and James Urquhart from the other side, presumably Canada; Charles Vallei from Saginaw, and many others.[50]   While the North West and

49.   *Wis. Hist. Colls.*, XIX, 237-8; 241.
50.   Askin's blotters and ledgers.   The following are traders mentioned: Jean Durette, Ebenezer Allen, Louis Barthe, Isaac Zeans, Gabriel Hunot, Joseph Campau, J. Cecire, Thos. Smith, Gervies Hodienne, Frank Fontenay, Madame

Miamis companies, Angus and Mackintosh, Todd and McGill, McTavish and Frobisher contracted numerous business deals with this Detroit firm.[51]

Here, too, competition had to be encountered, for the fur trade was still the all important occupation of the day in this western world; and there were few merchants who were not connected with it in some way or other. James Abbott, according to Leeson, was the first Englishman to open a trading establishment at the old post Detroit, and for a number of years the Abbott firm was closely identified with the early fur traders there.[52] In 1790 Robert Abbott left for the Indian country to solicit trade, where he remained until the company dissolved in 1798.[53] Other merchants like Montague Trimble, William Pauling, the Jacob and the Williams companies entered this field of commerce.[54] Alexander Mackenzie came hither in 1784 with a small adventure of goods, to stake his fortune in Indian trade, but being admitted as a partner in the North West Company, he left Detroit in the spring of 1785 for the Grand Portage.[55]

Michilimackinac was the abode of many traders who may be dismissed without comment, for theirs was the common lot of all; waging a strenuous fight to hold and maintain their own in the midst of many competitive forces.[56]

50. *Con.* Vissena, Isadore Peltier, Jacob Fisher, Gabriel Godfrey, Mrs. Hands, Jonathan Scheflin, Wm. Rayley, John McGregor, Pierre Moran, Jean Marie Beaubien, John McPherson.
51. *Ibid.*
52. Leeson, *Hist. Macomb Co.*, 187.
53. *Abbott Papers*, XXXIV, 1.
54. *Mich. Hist. Colls.*, XI, 461.
55. Mackenzie, *Voyages*, I, xviii.
56. See note 37.

Sault Ste. Marie, too, played her role in the trading world, but hers was a minor part; Askin had his establishment there,[57] so also the North West Company,[58] and traders came and went as in other marts, while a wealth of furs must have slipped by her doors on their way from the West to Eastern markets.

In 1780 a Montreal blacksmith, Andrew LeClaire, located at Fort St. Joseph and was there when the Spaniards attacked the fort. The garrison and employees were mustered out of service in 1781, but Antoine LeClaire came back and took up his abode at Parc au Vache, a few miles up the river from the old fort. There he built a cabin, bought furs of the Indians, and plied his trade. Andrew LeClaire, his father, left for Milwaukee in 1800, where he engaged in trade. Every spring he visited Detroit to purchase his own merchandise and some needed by William Burnette of St. Joseph and John Kinzie and Robert Forsyth of Chicago, carrying with him to market their furs, maple sugar, grease, and corn.[59]

Not only was there an increase of traders and more extensive trading operations at the old trading marts during this régime, but minor posts were springing up and assuming permanent form in various parts of Michigan. The story goes that seven Frenchmen had by 1790 entered St. Clair County and located on the Black River. William Lee Jenks claims that this is doubtful, as no record can be found of such location, with one exception, that of a Mr. Pettit, who was something of a dealer and fur trader.[60]   Patrick St.

57.   *Wis. Hist. Colls.*, XIX, 237-8.
58.   *Mich. Hist. Colls.*, XXXVII, 561.
59.   "St. Joseph Traders", in *New Era*, Dec., 1910.
60.   Jenks, *Hist. of St. Clair Co.*, I, 140-1.

Clair established a combined military and trading post in this county in 1765,[61] while Peter Brandamour and Denis Causlet pitched their trading camps within her borders.[62] Francis and Jerome Navarre, Charles and John Baptiste were pioneer traders of Monroe County. Here between 1783 and 1784 was founded Frenchtown by Joseph Pulier Benac; and the North West Company are supposed to have had at that place one of their important trading depots.[63] In Menominee a French Canadian, Chappee by name, established a trading post for one of the fur-trading companies, presumably the North Westers.[64] Joseph La Framboise, too, was by that time making his annual trips into Grand River Valley; but he had established no permanent post as yet, for he spent his winters at Michilimackinac.[65] These are a few of the posts that were beginning to dot Michigan territory; posts. which, unlike those of the previous régime, were not abandoned by their founders whenever more lucrative spots for trade were discovered, but remained as nuclei where little settlements took root in the next régime.

The harvest of furs, reaped by British traders in Michigan during this régime was no small item, especially after the war closed. That considerable trading was done even while it was in progress is evident, from the constant clamor of merchants for goods to be used in exchange and for means to transport their furs to market, and from the bitter strife

61. *American State Papers* (Indian Affairs), I, 747; *Western Travels*, VIII, 227n.
62. Andreas, *Hist. of St. Clair Co.*, 494.
63. Wing, *Hist. of Monroe Co.*, 38; *Mich. Hist. Colls.*, VI, 362.
64. *Mich. Hist. Colls.*, I, 264-5.
65. *Ibid*, XXX, 176-7.

between traders at posts like Michilimackinac to obtain the largest supply of these precious pelts. In 1778 Detroit and Niagara are said to have furnished one-fourth of the peltries exported from Canada,[66] and it is computed that this trade brought into the coffers of the former post about £100,000 annually. In 1796, 1910 packs passed from this post over the Niagara portage, in 1797, 2,616, and in 1798, 2,704.[67]

Michilimackinac added her share also of peltries for the Eastern markets. In 1784, four thousand packs were sent from this post and its dependencies.[68] In 1786, it comprehended nearly three-fifths of the trade of the upper country.[69] In 1790, most of the merchandise of the Missouri River trade was brought from there by British and Spanish traders,[70] and in 1797, 3,216 packs were shipped to the East.[71]

A study of the various account books of early traders will give some estimate of the kind of furs handled. The following is an entry in Burnett's ledger for June, 1796; sold 99 packs composed of: 5 bears, 5 pound beaver, 10 fishers, 58 cats, 74 doe, 78 foxes, 108 wolves, 117 otters, 183 minks, 557 bucks, 1,231 deer, 1,340 muskrats, and 5,587 raccoons.[72] The various accounts show that the beaver pelt was far on the decline, while

66. *Mich. Hist. Colls.*, XIX, 509.
67. *Mich. Hist. Colls.*, XXV, 202-3. This is spoken of as the trade about Detroit and toward the Illinois and the Mississippi, Detroit being the depot through which furs from the latter regions passed.
68. *Ibid*, XI, 442.
69. *Ibid*, 483-4.
70. *Ibid*, XXXVII, 516 (n. 16).
71. *Ibid*, XXV, 205.
72. Burnett's ledger, 1796-7.

muskrat and raccoon skins were sold in large quantities.[73]

So much for statistics, which show that the British traders in Michigan were not idle; and it behooved them to industriously gather harvests of furs as fast as they could, for the days of British sovereignty over this section were numbered. The patriot had triumphed. The loyalist had laid down his arms, and the treaty of peace had been signed; but the British trader continued to roam through Michigan forests, barter for Michigan furs, cheat the Michigan Indian, and swear at the incoming Yankee. This fur trade was too important an item in English commerce to be relinquished all of a sudden; too juicy a plum to drop into the lap of the victorious Americans. So posts like Michilimackinac and Detroit were held as British possessions, until after the signing of Jay's treaty in 1795.[74]

The English trader might remain in defiance of treaties or orders to leave, in those stripling days of Uncle Sam before he had won the respect of the nations of the Old World; but to shut out the energetic Yankee,

---

73. Approximately the following skins were sent out from St. Joseph according to the account book in the one year 1796-7; —, 117 beaver skins and 222 pounds of same, 97 fishers, 1,591 deer, 3,127 doe, 5,091 muskrats, 160 bears, 250 wolves, 1,250 red skin, 215 cats, 280 foxes, 517 mink, 2,899 bucks, 436 otter and 22,032 raccoon. This is only an approximate estimate of the amount sent out for some of the packs were mixed and hence could not be taken into account. Burnett's ledger, 1796-7.
For the years 1800-1801 the returns were thus: 9 beaver, 119 otter, 10 bear, 1 elk, 248 mink, 1,076 deer, 62 cat, 2,014 muskrat, 107 fox, 518 red skin, 5,603 raccoon. Burnett's day-book.
74. *Mich. Hist. Colls.*, XXXI, 253; *Jay's Treaty*, Art. II.

as eager and greedy for gain as himself, was another problem. He came, erected his little post, sought the Indian on the hunting ground, and pushed trade as hard as any Briton.

William Burnett, one of the first of these Yankee pioneer traders, came from New Jersey. It is thought that as early as 1776 he visited St. Joseph Valley, but there is no record of his locating there until 1791, when he built a warehouse for storing furs, maple sugar, and grain, at the mouth of the river near the site of the old post founded years before by La Salle.

Farther up the river he built another house which served as a residence and store room for merchandise used in the fur trade. He and a certain John Sayer brought a large assortment of goods from Montreal, and for some time traded peacefully, carrying quantities of furs to Michilimackinac.

The success of this alien Yankee was by no means a pleasing sight to the commandant at Michilimackinac; so he ordered him to come to that post and join the firm of McBeth and Grant for a monopoly of the St. Joseph trade. Burnett refused, upon which he was plainly told that he need not return to St. Joseph; whereupon, seeing that remonstrance would be in vain, he acquiesced and agreed to try it for one season. The following year he severed his connection with the firm, whereupon he was accused by them of having received wampum belts from the United States commandant. He was arrested, placed in the guard house at Michilimackinac, and sent by way of Detroit to Montreal. When he finally returned to his post, he found most of his property confiscated by his clerks; and what little remained he was forced to give to the

Indians, who now favored the English in preference to the American trader.

Other British traders had by this time invaded St. Joseph Valley and a bitter strife ensued between them and Burnett.   But this quick-witted Yankee fooled his British tormentors, for he wooed, won, and married Kakima, the daughter of the chief of the Potawatomi. This gave him an influence among the Indians that it was difficult for any British trader to undermine, so they left him in peace.   For many years he remained in this region trading with the savages, seldom leaving his home except when going to market, or when employed by the United States to serve them in adjusting their relation to the Indians over whom he had great influence.

Burnett led in person some of his expeditions on the St. Joseph and Kankekee rivers and made an annual trip to Michilimackinac or Detroit to dispose of the peltries or replenish his stock of merchandise. Commercially, he was connected with men like Jean Baptiste and John Kinzie of Chicago and James May of Detroit.   Three of his account books still in existence, covering a period from 1791 to 1802, show that he traded at Sault Ste. Marie, Michilimackinac, Grand river, and Chicago.[75]

The advent and successful operation of the American trader foreshadowed the pending doom of the British régime over the fur trade within Michigan territory.

75.   *Mich. Hist. Colls.*, XXX, 85-95.   A great deal of the material in this article is based upon an old document found among the Woodbridge Papers, *Burton Hist. Colls.*, Detroit; Baker, "Some Traders of St. Joseph Valley," pub. in *New Era*, Dec., 1910; see also Burnett's ledgers and day-book.

As early as 1785 the Montreal merchants realized that the Northwestern trade would soon be in the hands of the Americans. They had one advantage; they could afford goods cheaper and could give higher prices for peltries.[76] McGill, writing to John Askin, April 12, 1786, suggested that it might be the most proper time to dispose of their homes and lands, before the final determination of the United States Government was known concerning the posts, as he would not care, he said, to have dead business on his hands.[77] The Americans had begun to establish posts on the frontier near Detroit. This meant a falling off of trade south of Lake Erie and in the American territory, and if Detroit was obtained they feared that the whole of the Northwest trade would be lost.[78] Hence Montreal merchants in 1790 petitioned Lord Dorchester to make an effort to secure permission from the American Government to have five years for collecting and withdrawing their property.[79] When on July 11, 1796, Detroit was evacuated by British troops, the last vestige of British authority passed from Michigan lands; yet the British trader remained. The same treaty which had required him to give up her main posts, gave him the right of trading within her territory.[80] English traders remained, and it will be seen in the following chapters how English influence prevailed particularly around Michilimackinac until after the close of the War of 1812.

---

76. Brymner, *Canadian Archives*, 1890, 56-7.
77. *Askin Papers*, I, 167.
78. *Mich. Hist. Colls.*, XXIV, 163-4; Brymner, *Canadian Archives*, 1890, 56-58.
79. *Mich. Hist. Colls.*, XXIV, 162-4.
80. *Jay's Treaty*, Art. III.

CHAPTER VI

United States Policy and the Extension of Its Trade into Michigan

THE Michigan fur trade passed under three successive régimes — the French, the English, and the American; the first two have been treated, the last must now be considered. This latter period saw not only the "Golden Age" of Michigan's forest commerce but also its decline and destruction. It was a period of systematic, wholesale exploitation of the furred creatures of her forests by factory, fur-trading company, and independent trader, without thought of reservation or preservation; a period when the dollar took the place of the beaver pelt, salaries the place of the credit system, and the Yankee the place of the Briton; a period when her splendid forests and Indian hunting grounds were transformed into pastures and farms, and her trading rendezvous became the sites of villages and thriving cities; when the trapper and hunter and savage gave way to the man with the axe and the hoe, the lumberman, the merchant, and the farmer.

The factory, fur-trading company, and independent trader were all at work, each contending for the largest share of the spoils. The two latter existed during the British régime; the first named is a new element. The factory system was an attempt made by the United States to control the Indian trade by establishing trading houses under the supervision of government officials. The purpose was two-fold: to keep the savage supplied with merchandise, and to furnish him protection and justice against the greed and avarice of traders.[1] It had its origin in 1795, when Congress, to test the system, appropriated $50,000 to purchase goods for supplying the Indians in that year.[2] The following year they granted the President the privilege of forming such establishments throughout the country for the purpose of carrying on trade with the various tribes. He was to appoint agents for each trading house, whose duty it was to receive and dispose of the goods for the savages. All employees were required to take oath that they would not engage in any trade, commerce, or barter with the Indians except on public account; if they should, they were subject to a penalty of removal from office and forfeiture of $1,000. Not a drop of brandy, rum, or whiskey was allowed in these factories.[3]

Custom was to govern the price charged for merchandise, and no imperfect goods were to be sold to the Indians. All goods placed in the trading houses were for them alone, and if purchased by other persons, they were to be paid for, at an advance of ten per cent.[4]

1. McKenny, *Memoirs*, 18.
2. Washington's Message to Congress in 1795, in *Writings of Washington* (Ford ed.), XIII, 144-5; *U. S. Statutes at Large*, I, 443.
3. *Annals of the 4th Congress*, 2nd Sess., 2889-91. This Act was passed April 18, 1796. *U. S. Statutes at Large*, I, 452-3.
4. Indian letter-book, in *Wis. Hist. Colls.*, XIX, 326-30. The idea was to give him goods at cost prices. To gain the friendship of the Indians and inspire them with confidence in the honor, integrity and good faith of the Government.

The agents were to render accounts four times a year
for all goods and money passing through their hands.
In Michigan all accounts, vouchers, abstracts, and
estimates of these Indian agents were sent to the
Governor of the Territory for examination.[5] The Act
providing these trading houses remained in force only
two years. It was revived again in 1802 and retained
until 1822, when trading houses were finally abolished.[6]

5. Territorial Records, in *Mich. Hist. Colls.*, XXXVI, 557-61.
6. The following Acts relating to Indian trading houses have
        been passed:
    (1) An Act for establishing trading houses with Indian
            tribes, April 18, 1796. *U. S. Statutes at Large*, I,
            Chap. 13.
    (2) An Act to revive and continue in force "An Act for
            establishing trading houses with Indian tribes,"
            April 30, 1802. *Ibid*, II, Chap. 39.
    (3) An Act for continuing in force a law entitled, "An Act
            for establishing trading houses with the Indian
            tribes," Feb. 28, 1803. *Ibid*, Chap. 14.
    (4) An Act for establishing trading houses with the Indian
            tribes, April 21, 1806. *Ibid*, Chap. 48.
    (5) An Act supplemental to an Act entitled, "An Act for
            establishing trading houses with the Indian tribes,"
            March 3, 1809. *Ibid*, Chap. 34.
    (6) An Act establishing trading houses with the Indian
            tribes, March 2, 1811. *Ibid*, Chap. 30.
    (7) An Act to continue in force an Act entitled, "An Act
            for establishing trading houses with the Indian tribes,"
            March 3, 1817. *Ibid*, Chap. III, 43.
    (8) "An Act directing the manner of appointing Indian
            agents and continuing the Act for establishing trading
            houses with the Indian tribes," April 16, 1818.
            Ibid, Chap. 66.
    (9) An Act to continue in force for a further term the Act
            entitled, "An Act for establishing trading houses
            with the Indian tribes," March 3, 1819. *Ibid*,
            Chap. 80.
    (10) An Act to continue in force for a further time the Act
            entitled, "An Act for establishing trading houses
            with the Indian tribes," March 4, 1820. *Ibid*,
            Chap. 20.

Indian tribes within the jurisdiction of the United States were to be divided into departments, for each of which there was to be a Superintendent of Indian Affairs.[7] Every person wishing to carry on Indian trade had to secure a license from the superintendent of his department, or from any other person appointed by the President for that purpose. He must give $1,000 bond and have one or more sureties approved by the person issuing his license, and must promise to observe all rules and regulations. These licenses were granted for two years and might be revoked by the person issuing them if he found that they were violated. Anyone who attempted to trade without one, if convicted, should forfeit such merchandise as he had attempted to sell to the Indian tribes.[8] This system with slight modifications continued in force practically through the entire fur-trading régime in Michigan.

The following instructions were given to the licensed trader: He was to be confined to the place to which he was assigned, and was to deal "friendly and fairly" with the Indians; he was to attend no council held by them nor send them any speech accompanied by wampum; he must neither carry, nor sell, nor dispose of any liquor to them; if he did so, or attempted to

(11) An Act to continue in force for a further time the Act entitled, "An Act to establish trading-houses with the Indian tribes," March 3, 1821. *Ibid*, Chap. 45.

(12) The trading houses with the Indian tribes were abolished by "An Act to abolish the United States' trading establishment with the Indian tribes," May 6, 1822. *Ibid*, Chap. 54.

7. *U. S. Statutes at Large*, I, 4th Cong., 1st Sess., Chap. 30, sec. 7.

8. *Annals of 1st Congress*, II, 2241. Act approved July 22, 1790. *Ibid*, 137, Chap. 33.

trade without a license, they were authorized to seize his goods for their own use, a provision to be made known to the Indians; he must report any unlicensed trader who attempted to trade, and must try to impress upon the red men the necessity of living in peace among themselves and with the Yankee traders.[9] Thus by means of trading houses and the license system, the United States hoped to regulate and control trade. Hers was a policy differing from that of the two previous régimes in this respect, that her laws, at least, acknowledged that the rights of the original owners of the hunting grounds should be recognized and respected, as well as those of the traders.

So much for the policy of the United States. The history of Michigan's forest commerce during this period is the history of a gradual elimination of English influence by American up to the year 1812, when war called a halt to trade for a few years; after which British traders were barred from seeking peltries in American territory and British influence ceased. After the war this commerce was pushed to the utmost in certain regions and centers of trade until it reached its zenith. Then followed a period of decline, when the Indians through the influence of traders peacefully relinquished their hunting grounds to the incoming settlers. Such in brief is a survey of the entire period. We turn now to a more detailed consideration of that part of the régime when English influence predominated,—a period which lasted until after the War of 1812. That such a state of affairs should be possible

9. Instructions to Louis Campau, given at Detroit Nov. 15, 1833, by Wm. Woodbridge, in *Campau Papers*. See also instructions to Daniel Borassa, *Burton Hist. Colls.*, MS. Vol. CXV, 37.

was due partly no doubt to the freedom of trade within the American territory, which was granted to British subjects by Jay's treaty.[10]

James McGill prophesied that when English official rule in Michigan closed there would be no general oxodus of traders from Detroit, but that they would become American subjects so as to keep in their hands the trade.[11] This no doubt could have been said of the majority of the posts. A few loyal British removed into Canada, but the greater number remained, some of whom were suspected of sympathizing strongly with the English.[12]

In October, 1796, the United States took official possession of Michilimackinac,[13] but her forest commerce remained in the hands of British traders with their French and half-breed employees.[14] English influence was stronger and held its own there for a greater length of time than at Detroit, which was natural, for the main British trading post was close by, namely, at St. Joseph Island, and the majority of the British merchants maintained some establishment at Michilimackinac.[15] But more potent no doubt in maintaining English influence were the two great fur-trading firms, the North West and the Mackinaw companies whose members were largely British subjects, chiefly Scotchmen.[16] The latter com-

10. *Jay's Treaty*, Art. 3.
11. Brymner, *Canadian Archives*, 1890, p. 57.
12. *Mich. Hist. Colls.*, XXXVI, 416; *Ibid*, XXV, 250-58; *Wis. Hist. Colls.*, XVIII, 439-40.
13. *Wis. Hist. Colls.*, XIV, 12; *Ibid*, XVIII, 447-8; *Mich. Hist. Colls.*, XX, 466.
14. *Wis. Hist. Colls.*, XIV, 14.
15. *Wis. Hist. Colls.*, XVIII, 439n, and 447-8.
16. *Wis. Hist. Colls.*, XIV, 14; Chittenden, *Fur Trade of the Far West*, I, 310.

pany got a powerful hold on Michigan and Lake
Superior trade, so much so that John Jacob Astor,
who was anxious to obtain at least a portion of it,
realized that to oppose this concern would bring no
profit, hence he sought to neutralize its power by other
means.[17]

But the Michigan fur trade was gradually slipping
from British hands as conditions were becoming more
and more unfavorable; elements were creeping in and
events happening that were bound to drive the British
out.   One of these was the constant influx of American
traders, who threatened soon to outnumber the British.
In 1808 several arrived at Detroit, "a whole swarm of
Yankees," says John R. Williams, "mostly merchants
from Boston."[18]   Assuredly, Michilimackinac was also
sought by ambitious Yankee peltry dealers, though
at first their entrance was not in as great numbers as
at the lower post.   Two interesting characters who
figured prominently in the American régime and will
be spoken of later were Monsieur and Madame La
Framboise, who arrived at this post in 1802.   When
seven years later, with two boats and twelve men they
were proceeding to their usual wintering place on the
Grand River and Monsieur La Framboise was shot
by an Indian, his wife continued the journey, met the
savages at their bartering rendezvous and transacted
the usual business.   Later she returned to Michilimackinac, procured a license, and took up her
permanent abode in Grand River Valley.[19]   William
Burnett, one of the first Americans to pitch his trading

17. Chittenden, *Fur Trade of the Far West*, I, 309-10.
18. Williams Papers, in *Burton Hist. Colls.*, MS. Vol. XIX, 70.
19. *Wis. Hist. Colls.*, XIV, 38-41; *Mich. Hist. Colls.*, XVII, 326;
      XI, 193.

camp on St. Joseph River, continued to barter with the Indians of that section until 1804.[20] Joseph Bertrand also had a post there. For some time he was acting agent for a fur company, but in 1808 he went into business for himself and settled on the west side of St. Joseph River near the crossing of the Sac Trail, where he erected a log cabin and a fur press.[21]

The factories established in this section by the government, though at no time very potent forces in the fur trade, nevertheless served to increase American influence as against the British. In 1802 four new factories were provided for, among which was one to be placed at Detroit for the trade of the Northwestern tribes. But its existence in this post was short. Already, in 1804, it closed its doors and the government goods were sent to Chicago.[22]

In 1805 a movement was on foot to remove the trading factory from Ft. Wayne and Chicago to Michilimackinac. Opposition arose. Henry Dearborn held that such a step would prevent the Indians from securing supplies; that there were few red men around Michilimackinac, and, if the factory were placed there, those farther away would be forced to get their goods from British traders.[23] These arguments were swept aside; the factory was established in 1806 and Joseph B. Varnum was appointed United States agent for that place. A dwelling house and store was rented by the Secretary of War, for which the factor was to

---

20. *Mich. Hist. Colls.*, XXX, 92-95; "Some Fur Traders of St' Joseph Valley," *The New Era*, Dec. 1910.
21. "Some Fur Traders of St. Joseph Valley," *The New Era*, Dec. 1910.
22. *Wis. Hist. Colls.*, XIX, 311n.
23. Indian letter-book, in *Wis. Hist. Colls.*, XIX, 310-11.

pay a stipulated rent of $150. Mr. Irwin who was on his way to the factory at Chicago was ordered to leave 172 packages with goods and other necessary articles for the post.[24]

The king of early American fur traders, John Jacob Astor, did a great deal to neutralize the power of British traders within American territory. The American Fur Company, of which he was the chief and director, had been chartered in 1808. With all the confidence of a self-made man, its founder dreamed of harnessing the forest commerce of the West to that of the East and hold the reins himself. But a powerful British company, the Mackinaw, had firmly intrenched itself in one of the richest spots for fur trade, namely, the Lake region. For a newcomer to fight an old and strong firm was absurd, so he offered to purchase a share in it. The offer was accepted and a two-thirds interest in their trade within the United States was sold to Mr. Astor with the understanding that all of it was to come into his hands after five years.[25] This was a significant move in the game, for there can be no question that the strongest hold the British trader had on Michigan as well as the lake trade, was that held by the Mackinaw Company.

When the British saw that the passing of the southern posts of this territory into American hands was inevitable, the importance of holding Sault Ste. Marie was fully realized. Major R. Matthews, in 1790, suggested the use of this place for part of the Northwest

24. *Ibid*, 331-2, 333.
25. Chittenden, *Fur Trade of the Far West*, I, 309-11. The names of the Mackinaw traders in the company seem to have been Cameron, Fraser, Dickson and Rolette. *Ibid*.

trade in place of Michilimackinac, as furs could be brought from here down the Grand or the Ottawa River directly to Montreal. He held that the loss of Michilimackinac would rob them of the western trade unless a post like this could be kept.[26]

In 1798 a dispute which continued for years arose between some British firms which had trading interests there over the control of the Strait. The old North West Company had divided and the original firm applied for a grant of land at Sault Ste. Marie on which to erect certain improvements to facilitate trade. The granting of this was strongly opposed, particularly by the London agents of the XY Company. It was feared that this would be a detriment to others engaged in trade there. The Duke of Portland wrote to Gen. Peter Hunter, March 13, 1800, that he thought the possession of a tract of land in that place by any one firm would be highly injurious to others engaged in the fur trade. He said, "I am strongly inclined to be of the opinion that it must be very much for the benefit of the Fur Trade that about four or five leagues, or perhaps the whole of the strait in question forever should be retained in the hands of the crown."[27]

The request of the old North West Company, however, was granted, and they built a canal and constructed a road that they might, says Harmon, take up loaded canoes and not be under the necessity of carrying them by land to the head of the rapids. It seems that these improvements were finished by

26. Colonial Office Records, in *Mich. Hist. Colls.*, XXIV, 95.
27. Brymner, *Canadian Archives*, 1886, xxvi; papers from Canadian Archives, in *Mich. Hist. Colls.*, XXIII, 419.

1800 and the feud between the old and the new companies began; the XY Company claimed the right to use a canal built on public property, the old company held that this right could not be granted unless tolls were paid, and so the dispute continued.[28]

The attempt by the British to smuggle goods for the Indian trade into American territory, thus evading the revenue laws, helped considerably to increase the feeling of hostility between the two nations. By an Act of Congress of March 2, 1799, Michilimackinac and the region adjacent, including Sault Ste. Marie and Grand Portage, was made into a revenue district, of which the first-named post was to be the only port of entry, and a collector was appointed to levy duties upon the merchandise passing into the district.[29] This caused British firms like those of Forsyth, Richardson & Co., and Parker, Gerrard & Ogilvy considerable worry. A large cargo of goods was brought by them into American territory, but they had failed to go into the port of entry for the collection of duties. Rumor reached them that the American collector was coming to seize their merchandise, hence they petitioned General Peter Hunter, contending that no fraud whatever against the revenue office had been contemplated; that they had simply followed an old course, to go out of which would be ruinous to trade,

28. Masson, *Les Bourgeois*, II, 146-7; see also Brymner, *Canadian Archives*, 1886, xxviii; *Mich. Hist. Colls.*, XXIII, 422-3. Johnston in his account of Lake Superior says that in 1809 the old North West Company had a sawmill, several stores, and houses for the reception of their goods from Montreal, but makes no mention of the canal. Masson, *Les Bourgeois*, II, 146.

29. U. S. *Statutes at Large*, I, 638, Chap. 22, sec. 17.

and hence, innocently and unwittingly, had transgressed rules and regulations.[30]

But matters were fast approaching a crisis. The
irritation between the two powers was daily increasing.
In 1807 affairs assumed a serious aspect when a party
of American soldiers fired on a convoy of the Mackinaw
Company. This aroused the ire of the British.
Montreal merchants entered a strong protest against
such action. They claimed that long had they suffered
under the requirements of passes, extortions in the
shape of duties, and various other vexations, in viola-
tion of former treaty stipulations; a treaty which
claimed to maintain an equality among Indian traders
whether British or Americans. They said: "The
Indian trade within the American limits must speedily
be abandoned by British subjects, if not protected
against interruptions of free navigation of the Lakes,
fiscal extortions, and various other vexations: that if
once abandoned, it can never be regained and with
its abandonment, will finish British influence with the
Indian Nations residing within the limits of Canada:
that British Traders have materially aided in preserv-
ing that influence hitherto, the conviction of which is
the strong motive with the American Government for
wishing, by every means they can devise, to exclude
such traders."[31]

The American trader, too, had his grievances; not
only did the British rob him of a forest commerce
which he felt was rightfully his and smuggle in mer-

30. *Mich. Hist. Colls.*, XXIII, 425-428. McTavish, Frobisher
     and Company had by this time moved to the British side.
31. Memorial of Montreal merchants, in *Mich. Hist. Colls.*,
     XXV, 250-258.

chandise for exchange; but his influence over the red man was no small concern in this fur-trading world. In many places American traders were forced to be constantly on the alert against depredations of savage Indian tribes incited by the British to attack their helpless posts.[32]

So the hostility between the two trading factions grew, until the War of 1812 called both American and Briton from the hunting grounds and forced them to relinquish all schemes and plans for out-witting each other. When the war was over, American domination of Michigan fur trade became supreme. The English trader however did not entirely disappear; many of the chief traders and clerks of the American Fur Company were former British subjects, but they were now British subjects Americanized.

Trade was dull in those early years of the nineteenth century, a condition not confined to Michigan alone but rather general, in the fur-trading world.[33] In Detroit little money and an oversupply of merchandise was the status of affairs. John Askin prophesied "ruin to him who did not have a long purse well filled;"[34] and McGill declared, as early as 1798, that he would send no more goods thither, as more than usual had gone up and he feared that prices would

32. "Some Fur Traders of St. Joseph Valley," *The New Era*, Dec. 1910. Evans' Pedestrious Tour, in *Western Travels*, VIII, 222.

33. John Askin in a letter dated Jan. 18, 1800, spoke of the latest accounts from England as showing a bad appearance for furs. Many fur buyers were bankrupt, as several houses in Hamburg had failed, which caused the failure of several houses in New York and London. *Askin Papers*, VII, 221.

34. Askin Papers, in *Burton Hist. Colls.*, MS. Vol. VII, 24.

drop.[35] John R. Williams attributed the poor conditions of trade at Detroit to the strong competition
that arose because of the "swarm of Yankees from
Boston" who came there to trade.[36] Plenty of furs
were shipped out, to be sure. Forty thousand dollars·
worth were exported from the Detroit district in a
single quarter ending June 30, 1807, according to the
custom-house officials,[37] but with so many to share
the profit, little would go to each one. In 1801 a
large number of packs were brought to Michilimackinac
and shipped to Detroit, but the merchants refused to
receive them.[38]

John Mason complained of poor returns in the
factories on the lakes. He said that in 1809 the whole
quantity of sale of hatters' furs did not exceed 10,000
raccoon skins, 3,000 muskrats, and 40 or 50 beavers.[39]
The forest commerce was not yielding the rich returns
of the good old days, partly because trading conditions
were poor throughout the fur-trading world, and partly
because of the ruthless competition existing among

35. *Ibid*, V, 50.
36. Williams Papers, in *Burton Hist. Colls.*, MS. Vol. XIX, 70.
37. Woodbridge Papers, in *Burton Hist. Colls.*, MS. Vol. CV,
     107.
38. Askin Papers, in *Burton Hist. Colls.*, MS. Vol. IX, 151.
     The Factors in general complained of a hard winter, as
     preventing the Indians from hunting as much as usual.
     Morrison speaks of an indifferent hunt. Forsyth,
     Richardson & Company say in 1810: "Notwithstanding
     the favorable sales of Deer & Beaver we do not see that
     a loss on the whole business of the company can be avoid-
     ed" unless returns this year are great and sales are very
     favorable. *Wis. Hist. Colls.*, XIX, 337-8.
39. Askin Papers in *Burton Hist. Colls.*, MS. Vol. V, 245.

the vast numbers of men who sought to grow rich as peltry dealers.[40]

40. Quotations of fur prices are of little significance because of the constant fluctuation. However, in 1799 raccoons are quoted low; deer, beaver, otter, and bear skins high. In 1810 Mackinaw goods averaged as follows:

deer......... 7 — 2
beaver.......13 —
otter.........16 — 3
fisher.......... 7 — 33
33 bear......20 — 21
21 swan skin.30 —

while it was spoken of as difficult to sell raccoon and mink skins.   Askin Papers, in *Burton Hist. Colls.*, MS. Vol. V, 245; VII, 176; *Wis. Hist. Colls.*, XIX, 338.

CHAPTER VII

TRADE DURING THE WAR OF 1812 AND EARLY OPERATIONS OF THE AMERICAN FUR COMPANY

READILY can we imagine that when that far-sighted financial genius, John Jacob Astor, obtained a two-thirds share in the Mackinaw Company,[1] many schemes for immediate gain in this most fruitful field for forest commerce were revolving in his mind. But if such plans were formed by him, he was doomed to disappointment because the War of 1812 began and brought the great fur business to a standstill. Capt. Charles Roberts, a British officer stationed on St. Joseph Island, gathered together an impromptu army composed of his garrison, a few Indians, and some traders, and before the Americans could hinder it seized Michilimackinac.[2] This was a blow to the trade of the Americans, for the British whose influence with the Indians was already strong were thus able to secure their alliance and trade as well as their assistance against Detroit.

To Astor it threatened to mean a heavy financial loss, for not only had he a large quantity of furs stored there at the time, but many Michilimackinac traders, —in fact, he said, nearly all of them,— were more or less indebted to him. Steps were at once taken to save the situation and obtain at least a part if not all

1. *Mich. Hist. Colls.*, VI, 343; XXXVI, 73-4; Irving, *Astoria*, 54-55; Chittenden, *Fur Trade of the Far West*, I, 309-11.
2. *Mich. Hist. Colls.*, XV, 110.

the credit that had been granted. Ramsay Crooks, a man almost if not quite as keen, active and ambitious as his employer, was ordered to proceed thither, that he might be on the spot when the returns were brought in from the hunting grounds. But little, practically nothing could be done. These were not days for trade. In 1813 he was able to purchase only a few skins. British merchants had none and, as far as the Americans were concerned, he could depend only upon what small parcels the inhabitants had been fortunate enough to conceal in previous years. Moreover, the dwellers at Michilimackinac, not foreseeing that war was nigh, had neglected importing any Indian goods during the last summer, and when the British advanced upon Malden they destroyed every cent's worth belonging to the Government,—a dark outlook indeed for men in the fur business.[3]

Not only was there practically no merchandise at this post for Indian trade but there was little prospect of securing any, because positive commands had been sent out from the Navy Department that navy officers should carry no private property whatever on their vessels, be it fur or merchandise.[4] Nothing daunted, Ramsay Crooks wrote Astor to secure if possible a temporary suspension of that rule, as otherwise there would be no fur trade in Michilimackinac that year. Astor went to Washington in the spring of 1814 and obtained permission for a private vessel to go to the post and bring away the packs of fur and other belongings of the South West Company, which were partly his property and partly that of British subjects.[5]

---

3. Crooks' letter-book, 12, 16-17.
4. *Ibid*, 22-25.
5. *Ibid*, 16-17, 32-34, 72.

At the same time he sent George Astor to Montreal to secure a permit from Montreal authorities.[6]

But George Astor had no more than performed his mission, and secured the schooner *Union*, with which to carry away the company's peltries at Michilimackinac, when a new obstacle was encountered. American forces had captured St. Joseph Island, and news reached him that all the goods of the South West Company had been seized.[7] Matters however terminated better than was expected under the circumstances. On June 9, 1814, Lieutenant George Prevost of Montreal ordered that vessels carrying a flag of truce and a passport should be allowed to go to the Isle du Bois Blanc near Michilimackinac, to receive on board skins and furs belonging to either Astor, Messrs. McTavish, McGilivray & Co., or Forsyth, Richardson & Co. Lists of the goods belonging to each of these were to be made out by their agents, passports to be furnished at Michilimackinac, and the boats were free to pass unmolested to the posts designated in the pass.[8] Thus they were enabled to send packs already on hand to market; but to obtain new ones was a different proposition. The outlook for the fur business was and continued to be so poor at Michilimackinac that Ramsay Crooks advised Astor to make no preparations for trade in that place.[9]

After the Americans had captured St. Joseph Island in 1813 and destroyed the buildings of the North West Company at that place, they thought wise to send a detachment to Sault Ste. Marie to accord a similar

---

6. *Ibid*, 82-3.
7. *Ibid*.
8. McArthur Papers, in *Wis. Hist. Colls.*, XIX, 354.
9. Crooks' letter-book, 32-34, 38-40.

treatment to this company's property there. Rumors
had reached them that John Johnston, acting as the
company's agent, had on hand a large quantity of
their goods and provisions which he gave to hostile
Indians.[10] The buildings of this firm were on the
British side. Here dwelt some old Canadian boatmen
with their half-breed wives and children, also a Charles
Emalinger, one of the wealthiest traders at the Sault,
a man according to Bigsby who was "every inch a
trader, public-spirited, skilful, sanguine and in-
defatigable."[11] On the American side were the homes
of Mr. Johnston and the old Indian trader Nolin.[12]

The troops landed on the British shore near the
establishment of the North West Company. Immediately they proceeded to the other side to call to
account John Johnston, the supposed agent of the
firm. He was absent at the time, but his son firmly
declared that neither he nor his father had ever been
an agent of the company or the Government, and that
all the goods he had on hand were private property.
Either the soldiers were bent on plunder or they felt
that the accusations against him were not without
foundation, for they emptied his stores, cellars, and
apartments of their contents. Then the warehouses
of the company were pillaged and set on fire.[13] These

10. Memoir of Johnston, in *Mich. Hist. Colls.*, XXXVI, 66.
11. Franchère's Narrative, in *Western Travels*, VI, 395n.
12. *Ibid*, VI, 394-5.
13. Memoir of John Johnston, in *Mich. Hist. Colls.*, XXXVI,
      67-68. Schoolcraft says, "This statement so far as
      respected Mr. Johnston's having in charge goods for the
      North West Company, or having any commercial con-
      nexion whatever with that company, was wholly ground-
      less. Nor did he at that, or any other time, permit prop-
      erty to be issued from his stores to Indians except in the
      usual mode of exchange for furs." *Ibid*, XXXVI, 66.

were anxious days for the North Westers, as a million
dollars' worth of fur was on its way from the Interior,
and they were fearful lest at any time that rich cargo
should fall into the enemy's hands. Happily, the
dreaded foe was absent when the forty-seven canoe
loads, laden with precious peltries, arrived and passed
by Sault Ste. Marie to the Eastern market, all un-
beknown to the unsuspecting Yankee.[14]

In the meanwhile, Detroit, Michigan's southern
trading mart, was a scene of Indian turmoil.[15] Com-
modore Perry tried to bring order out of the existing
chaos and make a treaty of peace with those most
actively engaged in war in Detroit and its environs.
This he succeeded in doing, and quiet was restored
at least for a time.[16] Astor, seeing there was no
prospect for trade in Michilimackinac, ordered Crooks
to proceed to this post, thinking that a few furs, at
least, if not money might be obtained.

There were stored here a few raccoon and muskrat
pelts, but to transact any business and profit by it was
an impossibility. The scarcity of peltries led those
who had any at all to demand the most exorbitant
prices for them. "I think it the height of folly,"
wrote Crooks, "to try to bring these lunatics to their
senses, and after stating the prices I would give, I
have left them to their own reflections for a few days."
Shrewd, keen, business man that he was, he could
accomplish nothing. Not only did the merchants
demand cash payments, refusing notes or drafts of
any kind, but they also placed their prices so high,

14. Franchère's Narrative, in *Western Travels*, VI, 395-97.
15. Crooks' letter-book, 16, 56-8; Evans' Pedestrious Tour, in
    Western Travels, VIII, 223-5.
16. Crooks' letter-book, 16.

that he saw a bargain could only be made at a loss to his firm. He therefore left Detroit.[17]

Though the War of 1812 played havoc with the fur trade at the principal posts, to Ramsay Crooks it appeared a God-send for the interests of the Astor Fur Company. He saw in it not only an opportunity to establish permanent trade in this section but to secure preponderance over all other concerns. With the fall of British influence, the monopoly of trade which hitherto had been theirs, particularly in the Michilimackinac region, would go to the Astor Company. "It seems almost superfluous to add" wrote he to John Astor, "that you must be well aware how propitious and inviting the present crisis is, and what a powerful influence such an undertaking would have, in producing an instantaneous and amicable adjustment of all your outstanding concerns in that quarter."[18]

Crooks' prophecy became a reality. When war operations ceased and trade began to rally, the American Fur Company assumed enormous proportions, extending its influence through the entire Northwest to the Pacific Coast and south to the Gulf. Improved methods of trade were introduced, and Michigan commerce in peltries was pursued with new and increased vigor.

These were the last days of the great North Westers, who had so long held sway over the western forests and boldly extended their operations wherever it might be done with profit, in spite of territorial rights,

17. *Ibid.*
18. *Ibid.*

or other companies or other traders.[19]   After the war
came the final blow to British influence over United
States trade.   Congress, in 1816, largely it is thought
through Astor's influence, restricted her fur trade to
her own citizens.[20]   That year the South West Company passed out of existence,[21] and its interests, as
well as the agents, clerks, and departments of the
North West Company, were turned over to the Astor
Company.   This was reorganized as the American
Fur Company, and trade went on with light interruptions.[22]   A new and if possible a more intricate
and powerful organization was taking the place of
the fur magnates of former days; the old trader was
passing away, to be followed by the progressive Yankee.

Directly after the war, the district on the southern
shores of Lake Superior was tendered to Mr. John
Johnston, but this arrangement was closed when the
company reorganized in 1816.[23]   The region around
the Great Lakes was then made into a northern department and placed under the charge of Ramsay
Crooks and Robert Stuart.[24]   Crooks spent most of the
summer of 1817 at Michilimackinac organizing the

19.   Alexander Henry in a letter to John Askin expressed his
        regret at the passing away of the old traders.   He says,
        "I experience every day the want of old acquaintances.
        They are all dead .... What do you think of our Beaver
        Club?   In 1786 there were sixteen members and I the
        only one alive....late friend McGill was the last."
        Askin Papers, Burton *Hist. Colls.*, MS. Vol. CCCCLVII,
        1.
20.   *U. S. Statutes at Large*, III, 332, Chap. 165.
21.   Memoir of Johnston, in *Mich. Hist. Colls.*, XXXVI, 73-4;
        see also p. 74n.
22.   Memoir of Johnston, in *Mich. Hist. Colls.*, XXXVI, 73;
        Minn. Hist. Colls., V, 382.
23.   *Mich. Hist. Colls.*, 73-4.
24.   *Ibid*, VI, 346-7; XXXVI, 74 (n. 36).

124 MICHIGAN FUR TRADE

business.[25] More intimately connected with this little post was Robert Stuart, who spent here eighteen years in the company's service.[26] When he assumed the chieftainship of this section, he mapped out the entire country under his supervision, grouping every tribe and band into definite districts. Trading posts were to be established at every important point with a trader to manage each center, and out-stations to head off any opposition trader already in the field.[27]

At Michilimackinac, brigade companies were organized consisting of from five to twenty batteaux laden with goods. These were sent to the various districts of trade until the whole ground was occupied by the company's traders. Each clerk had his territory assigned before he started, so no interference of one with the other was liable to occur.[28]

Another element in their policy was to destroy the independent trader, by fair means or foul. If he could be bought out or attached to the company, well and good. If that plan did not work, underselling or some other means was resorted to, so that it is estimated that in the first year of their operation they brought into their employ seven-eighths of the old traders on the upper Mississippi, the Wabash and Illinois rivers, and Lakes Michigan and Superior.

The gigantic operations of this company may perhaps be best realized by noting the number of its traders and the regions into which its influence penetrated. In the study of the "outward invoices" of this company, made from Michilimackinac during the years

25. Chittenden, *Fur Trade of the Far West*, I, 312.
26. Bingham, *Michigan Biographies*, 621-2.
27. *Mich. Hist. Colls.*, III, 58; VI, 346-7; XXXVII, 134.
28. *Ibid*, XXXV, 66.

1821 and 1822, the following list of traders is found connected with it under various relations: Seven are working in joint account with the company, thirty-two secured supplies from them and were working on their own account and risk, three directly for the account of the company, and twenty-two for the account and risk of the company, a total of sixty-four traders, directly or indirectly connected with this concern.[29]

Undoubtedly, each one of these had employed several men in the sections where he was carrying on trade. For the year 1818-19, 277 employees exclusive of traders are listed in service, men scattered throughout various places and receiving wages of from $140 to $2,400 annually.[30]

The upper and lower Mississippi, Illinois, Wabash, Iroquois, and Kankakee rivers with their dependencies; the various parts of Wisconsin; the regions surrounding Lakes Huron, Superior, and Michigan, Ontario and

29. Outward Invoices, A. F. Co. "B," *Wis. Hist. Colls.*, XI, 371-77. Michigan had the following traders connected with the company; those trading on their own account and risk were: Antoine Deschamps, at Muskegon; Mrs. La Framboise, securing goods from Rix Robinson on the Grand River; Rix Robinson on Lake Michigan; William Farnsworth in the latter's employ; Thérèse Schindler, Joseph Rolette, R. M. Prior, Edward Biddle, Joseph C. Deschenaux, Ignace Picket, Eliza and William Mitchel, Jean St. Beaubien, James Kinzie, Joseph Bailly and Pièrre Caune at or in the vicinity of Michilimackinac. On the account and at the risk of the American Fur Company, the following are noted: Goodrich Warner and John Holliday at L'Anse and dependencies, Joseph Bertrand and Pièrre Navarre at St. Joseph and dependencies, James Abbott at Detroit and Madam La Framboise on the Grand River.

30. A. F. Co's. account books, 1818-19, in *Wis. Hist. Colls.*, XII, 154-169.

Drummond Island were canvassed for furs by this company's traders and clerks.[31]

Many peltries were brought to this little Michigan town, Michilimackinac, the central station for one of the most powerful trading concerns within the States.[32] Doubtless, better bargains could be made here in this common gathering place of peltry dealers. Then, too, the Indians had by this time developed a taste for certain kinds of merchandise which could be obtained in no other place except in New York and Montreal. These were the Mackinac blankets and certain kinds of strouds and calicoes, particular manufactures, made and imported only by persons engaged in the trade. The Indians, who in pioneer days were the white man's dupes, exchanging costly furs for mere trifles, had undergone an education. They had become excellent judges of the quality of articles which were imported to them, and readily ascertained the lowest prices for which they might be purchased.[33] Articles of inferior quality were contemptuously called American; this was due to the fact that goods of that kind had been sold to them at the United States factories.

Doubtless when they wished to purchase goods of the very best quality, they visited Michilimackinac. There in the months of July and August thousands of people, both savages and traders, gathered from various parts of the Indian country, some to deposit their furs, others to secure new outfits for the next hunt.

31. *Ibid.*
32. Detroit *Gazette*, Dec. 15, 1820.
33. *Ibid*, Dec. 22, 1820.

CHAPTER VIII

MICHIGAN FUR TRADE AT ITS HEIGHT

BY 1816 the British trader had been shut out from Michigan forests, and British influence was a thing of the past; the American Fur Company, fully organized, had mapped out its territory and sent out its chieftains with their little armies of traders while its posts and outposts were beginning to dot the river banks in every section of the Territory; the independent trader had pitched his camp in the most favorable spot for opposition; both he and the company were ready to begin in earnest to strip the forests of every furred animal that could be found. "Kill as long as there is to kill," seemed to be their motto. At least that is what they did. The enterprising Yankee invaded every haunt of the wild creatures of the woods, and robbed them of their fur folk, until some kinds became almost extinct and others extremely rare.

Of the two agents of trade mentioned, the strongest and the one exerting the greatest influence and amassing the largest gains was the company. But it was far from having an open field. Everywhere, it met the independent trader, and how to kill the "Opposition" was an ever-present problem, involving it in endless difficulties. Its policy was to crush, at whatever cost, those whom it could not buy. Usually it picked out its best traders, had them pitch their tent near the enemy and proceed to undersell him. To annoy the rival in trade seemed at times of more importance than the trade itself, and violent measures were often used. To create hostile relations between him and the Indian was a most potent means of destroying his trade. This was done through coaxing or threatening the latter, loading him with presents, appealing to his pride, and black-mailing the enemy. The savages were not adverse to having an opposition trader in their midst for it proved a profit to them. So bitter a feeling existed at times among the traders and clerks that in order to hold the allegiance of the Indians they gave them more than they would have gotten under different circumstances. A letter written by William Johnston in 1833 shows somewhat the attitude assumed by the American Fur Company and the independent trader toward each other. He says:[1] "The chief trader of the American Fur Company has arrived. He caused some stir among his men and the Indians belonging to his party; and with great ceremony he invited all the Indians to hold a talk—numbers attended, and from what they told me of his speech, he must have considered himself a little superior to the President himself, and he felt as gifted with papal authority to anathamatize his opposition and the Indians who should forsake his interests." Thus company and trader waged an interesting contest on the Indian hunting ground, but doubtless their treatment of each other was not a whit more blameworthy or shadowy than that of the great commercial rivals of today in their mad race for wealth.[2]

1. Adapted from Johnston's letters on the fur trade, in *Mich. Hist. Colls.*, XXXVII, 199-200.
2. For methods and policies of the opposition see: Mackenzie, *Voyages*, I, x, xviii; Perrault's Narrative, in *Mich. Hist. Colls.*, XXXVII, 562-3, 564-5; Johnston's letters on the

So much for the relation of these agencies of trade to each other, their main operations within Michigan Territory were largely confined to six prominent fur-trading sections, namely Michilimackinac, Detroit, and Sault Ste. Marie with their dependencies, and St. Joseph, Grand River, and Saginaw valleys. Besides these posts in the more important regions, others were scattered through the various parts of Michigan.

A region most fertile for trade was that of the Grand River Valley. It has been seen, that long before the War of 1812 and before the emigrant's coming, it had been sought by men in quest of furs. Langlade and his assistants came during the English régime; Monsieur and Madame La Framboise in the early days of the American; not to speak of the many temporary rovers of the French period who unquestionably met and traded here. Already its commerce in peltries had been of no small importance.[3] It was to yield a richer harvest to the American trader.

The American Fur Company with Rix Robinson as agent and sole manager had by 1827 established no less than twenty trading posts in this section. These commenced at Kalamazoo on the south and extended to Little Traverse on the north. In Grand Haven, their headquarters, they had a store, a warehouse,

2. *Con.* fur trade, in *Mich. Hist. Colls.*, XXXVII, 143, 145, 151-4; 156-7, 167-85, 188, 201. Chittenden, *Fur Trade of the Far West*, I, 344-5, 353, 367-8. For an interesting encounter of Rix Robinson with an agent of the Hudson Bay Co. see *Mich. Hist. Colls.*, XI, 190-2. Indians strongly took sides, preferring to go without numerous articles rather than purchase of the "Opposition." *Mich. Hist. Colls.*, XXXVII, 185, 188.

3. *Mich. Hist. Colls.*, XXX, 185.

17

and a dwelling house.[4] Closely linked with the fur trade of this valley, and particularly, with that of the counties of Kent, Ionia, and Ottawa, are the names of La Framboise, Robinson, Marsac, Campau, and Winsor. These men rendered their nation and their state an important service and played their part in the frontier world by paving the way for the future settler.

Woman,[5] too, had a hand in the forest trade of Grand River Valley, for one of the first representatives of the American Fur Company there, was a half-breed Ottawa woman; the annual visits to that place made by Monsieur La Framboise and his wife have already been noted, and the fact that on one of these trips he was shot by an Indian;[6] his wife, hardened by constant coping with frontier life, and perhaps because of the touch of Indian blood in her veins, was not daunted but proceeded to their usual place of trade and took up the work of her husband. She was so successful and on such friendly terms with the Indians, that the American Fur Company, ever on the lookout for able traders, employed her as their agent for this section.[7] She was a woman, says Thwaites, "of

4. *Ibid*, IX, 235-37.
5. A few women traders are mentioned in the Askin blotters and ledgers, and the Williams Brothers employed Indian women to collect furs.
6. Some held that he was shot while on his knees at prayer; others that the Winnebagoes killed him on a trading trip in Wisconsin. *Wis. Hist. Colls.*, XI, 373 (n. 2); there is another story that an Indian asked for whiskey, and when La Framboise refused he stabbed him with a knife. *Mich. Hist. Colls.*, XXX, 177.
7. *Mich. Hist. Colls.*, XXX, 176-7; *Ibid*, XI, 193; XVII, 325-326. Richmond, "The Fur Traders of the Grand River Valley" in the *Publications* of the Historical Society of Grand Rapids, I, Pt. III, 37.

commanding form, agreeable manners, and excellent
deportment; and highly esteemed by both whites and
Indians;" and G. S. Hubbard of Chicago spoke of her
as one "of extraordinary ability."[8] She remained in
the company's employ until 1821, when she removed
to Michilimackinac and Rix Robinson was chosen to
take her place.[9]

This chief of the Grand River fur traders was one
of the ablest clerks of the American Fur Company
and a conspicuous figure in the pioneer history of this
valley. He was not an unlearned man, for he had
studied the profession of law, but during the War of
1812 he came west as sutler to the United States
troops and, while thus employed, became interested
in the fur trade. With the soldiers he wandered to
Detroit, Michilimackinac, and Green Bay, all centers
of peltry traffic, where he had ample opportunity to
study its operations at first hand. Evidently, traffic

8. *Wis. Hist. Colls.*, XI, 373-4n. The American Fur Company
    in 1817-18 brought from Montreal a great number of
    clerks, among them Col. G. S. Hubbard, then a lad of
    sixteen. He reached Mackinac July 4, 1818. From there
    he proceeded to Chicago. In 1828 he purchased the
    entire interests of the fur company in Illinois. *Mich.
    Hist. Colls.*, III, 125-6; V, 14; VI, 344; XIV, 544-5.
9. In the invoices, made by the American Fur Company, she
    is listed as trading for them on their account and risks
    as late as September 3, 1821. Some goods were also
    delivered her, by them, in the summer of 1822. See "Sun-
    dry merchandise, from her inventory of Grand river Out-
    fit, 1821," for the account of Rix Robinson. *Invoices Out-
    ward.* A. F. Co. "B," *Wis. Hist. Colls.*, XI, 373-4, 376.
    The Chapman History of Kent County (p. 187) locates
    her hut in sec. 9, Lowell Township, Kent Co.   Thwaites
    says, "Her chief station....was at the site of Grand
    Rapids, Michigan, where she erected a trading hut, the
    first building in Kent County." *Wis. Hist. Colls.*, XI,
    374n.

in furs was more enticing than a lawyer's fee, for when the troops were mustered out of service he entered the Indian trade.

Two trading posts are supposed to have been established by him in Illinois; one at Calumet near the head of Lake Michigan, and one twenty-five miles from the mouth of the Illinois River. He had another at Milwaukee, Wisconsin, and two in Grand River Valley, Michigan. The latter were not independent posts, but belonged to the American Fur Company and were under Robinson's management.

This firm had other opposition besides that of the independent trader. The agents of the Hudson Bay Company caused them considerable annoyance. Several miles from St. Peter's River was a post established by this powerful rival, from which place, hitherto, every alien trader had been driven.

John Jacob Astor meeting Robinson at Michilimackinac in 1818 thought he saw in him the very qualities needed for a good opposition man to fight the agent of his rival. The post was offered to Robinson who gladly accepted it. He was fitted out and with his stock was transported to the designated spot where he was left without a companion in the midst of hostile Indians and more hostile traders. Now began an interesting boycott. The Indians often passed near his door on their way to trade at the enemy's post, but all efforts on his part to make a bargain proved futile. The old chief took particular delight in annoying him. Time and again he came brandishing his sword and shaking a package of fur at him. Finally Robinson's patience gave out as the old chief's insolence increased. The difficulty was settled in a fight in which the red man was beaten. After the pipe of peace had been smoked, the American Fur Company's agent succeeded in getting considerable trade, so that in the spring, when he returned to Michilimackinac he carried with him several packs.

When Madame La Framboise retired from the service of the American Fur Company, Robert Stuart who was then their manager at Michilimackinac invited Robinson to take charge of their posts on the Grand, the Kalamazoo, and the Muskegon rivers. He accepted the offer and took possession of the post previously in charge of Madame La Framboise. Later he established other posts on the Flat, Muskegon, Kalamazoo, and Grand rivers.[10]

Perhaps it is possible to form some idea of what sort of life these solitary frontier heroes led when we note that often for days he paddled his canoe on the rivers or traversed the forests alone seeking peltries for his firm. To be sure he had clerks and voyageurs assisting him, but their duties called them elsewhere. Zenas G. Winsor tells how when a mere youth, he came to enter Robinson's employ. His, too, must have been an interesting time, for he had as his assistants four French voyageurs and a half-breed girl, while he himself could speak neither the French nor the Indian tongue.[11]

Most of Robinson's sales were made and his supplies obtained at Michilimackinac. The annual departure and arrival of his fleet of batteaux were, no doubt, as important a break in the monotony of frontier life

10. *Mich. Hist. Colls.*, XI, 190-4.
11. *Mich. Hist. Colls.*, IX, 235; *Ibid*, 237, 243.

in Grand River Valley, as was the arrival of canoes of the North Westers at the Sault.[12]

Of all the employees of the great American Fur Company, there was perhaps no one who lived more peacefully with the independent traders than did Rix Robinson. At least, if any feuds existed in this section between them and Robinson, they have not been recorded. That he was a friend of the Indians is certain and, perhaps, he felt that harmony and peace among traders would serve the interests of his firm far more than war with the opposition. That he could fight we know from his encounter with the agent of the Hudson Bay Company; that there might have been plenty of opportunity to fight can not be questioned, because numerous independent traders established their posts in this section. These came largely from Detroit. Some were sent by merchants of this lower post to compete with the Mackinaw firm, and others came of their own accord.

Among the latter was Louis Campau, whom the

---

12. For Robinson's career see: *Mich. Hist. Colls.*, XI, 186-200; XIII, 575-76; IV, 287; IX, 241-2, 280; Richmond, *Fur Traders of Grand River Valley*, 37-39; *Wis. Hist. Colls.*, II, 152; The Chapman *Hist. of Kent Co.*, 184-209; *Wis. Hist. Colls.*, XI, 373-4.

In 1887 a monument was placed at Ada in memory of Rix Robinson by the Old Settlers' Association of the Grand River Valley. It bears on its sides the inscription: "In memory of Rix Robinson, born 1792, died 1875. Indian trader on Grand River, 1821. Supervisor Township of Ada, 1840; Associate Judge of Circuit Court for Kent County, 1844; State Senator, 1845; State Commissioner of Internal Improvements, 1846; Member of State Constitutional Convention, 1850. Brave, honest, patriotic, a loving husband and father, a friend of the Indians, their negotiator with the government and a peace maker." *Mich. Hist. Colls.*, XIII, 575-6.

townsmen called "Uncle Louis," and the Indians "Wa-gu-she," or the fox, because, said they, he was foxy in his dealings with them in early days.[13] He established posts and placed agents at Muskegon, Manistee, Kalamazoo, Lowell, Hastings, and Eaton Rapids, while he and Rix Robinson are each supposed to have had a sub-post at the mouth of Grand River, occupied only certain times of the year when shipments were made.[14] That an independent trader starting with little, perhaps no capital, was able to establish and maintain so many posts and amass, as he did, a fortune of $100,000,[15] shows to what extent men pushed the forest commerce in those days. If this was done by a single trader, what must have been the fortune amassed by a powerful concern like the American Fur Company.

Not only was the great Mackinac firm of the upper post and the independent trader at work in this field, but lesser associations at the post of Detroit sent their men thither to gather furs. Antoine Campau came to the Rapids in 1835 as an employee of the fur dealers, Pièrre Choteau, Jr., & Co., of New York City, and Buhl

13. *Mich. Hist. Colls.*, IX, 236. Likewise they called Rix Robinson Wa-Va-ohase, meaning marten, a fine furred, valuable animal; Col. Amos Roberts, Paga-nug-a-zische, or "big belly," because he was fat. Winsor they called, at first, Che-mo-ke-maness, or young Englishmen; later No-ba-quon, a vessel, "because," says he, "of a transaction they supposed me connected with, in a cabin of a small vessel then lying at our pole dock." *Ibid.*

14. Campau Papers, *Burton Hist. Colls.*, Detroit; Everett, *Mem. of Grand River Valley*, 10; Richmond, *Fur Traders of Grand River Valley*, 39-44; Schenck, *Hist. of Ionia and Montcalm Co.*, 29; *Mich. Hist. Colls.*, IV, 288; IX, 235; XVII, 320, 326; XXIX, 504.

15. Richmond, *Fur Traders of Grand River Valley*, 39-44; *Mich. Hist. Colls.*, XXX, 294.

& Co. of Detroit. The former soon transferred their business to the latter firm, who retained Campau in their services.[16]

Numerous other traffickers in the Grand River fur trade might here be mentioned; there was Richard Godfroy, "Jacquence," or little Joseph, as the savages called this Indian agent who, in 1837, placed the first steamboat on Grand River in the interest of trade, making regular trips to Lowell, Grand Haven and Muskegon;[17] there was Martin Ryerson, who saw more profit in felling the forest than its furred creatures, hence changed from fur king to lumber king;[18] Louis Generau, the half-breed, who plied the Grand for several years with his trading batteau;[19] John Baptiste Recollect, who built the first trading post in Muskegon,[20] and many others.[21]

With so many traders, representing different

16. Richmond, *Fur Traders of Grand River Valley*, 44-46.
17. *Mich. Hist. Colls.*, IV, 288; V, 438; VI, 331-2, XIII, 223. Richard Godfroy came from a family of traders; the Godfroy family are said to have been in the trading business as early as 1770, when his grandfather Jacques Godfroy was connected with the firm Godfroy and Beaugrand, who had trading firms between Ft. Vincennes and Monroe. For some years before coming to Grand Rapids he was Indian agent at the mouth of Flat River. *Ibid.*
18. *Mich. Hist. Colls.*, I, 291-3; XIII, 224, 219.
19. *Ibid*, I, 193; X, 161; Schenk, *Hist. and Directory of Kent Co.*, 65.
20. *Mich. Hist. Colls.*, I, 286.
21. Joseph Bailey at the mouth of Grand River and Étienne Lamorandie on Muskegon Lake, *Mich. Hist. Colls.*, XVI, 328; *Ibid*, XXVI, 272-3. Pièrre Constant, Joseph Daily, Louis Baddeau, William Lasley, George Campau, and Joseph Troutier in Muskegon. *Ibid*, I, 286, 291. Among the roll of employees for the American Fur Company in 1818, it is noted that a mason and a boatman were engaged for the Muskegon region. *Wis. Hist. Colls.*, XII, 154-169.

interests, it is not surprising that they did not wait
for the savage to bring his furs to the various posts,
but sent men directly to the Indian camps for them.
Thus Grand Haven, Allegan, Saugatuck, Gun Lake,
Gull Prairie, Thorn Apple River, Lyons, and Looking
Glass regions were visited, and canvassed over and
over again for furs.[22]

While all was peaceful and quiet along the Grand
River, a different scene was enacted in the Saginaw
Valley. Here a bitter contest was waged between
independent traders and the American Fur Company.
The latter had established a post in 1824 near the
present site of Saginaw, a spot which for years had
been the camping ground of Indians.[23]   Here was their
central depot for this section, and several outposts
were scattered along the river banks throughout the
valley. William McDonald who first had charge of
the station succeeded in securing a strong hold on the
trade here,[24] and his successor Eleazer Jewett was able
to maintain that position.[25]   Not so the Frenchman,
Patrice Réaume.[26]

Several independent traders had located in the
vicinity, among whom was Louis Campau. This man,
formerly a voyageur, had been engaged by some
Detroit merchants to go among the Saginaw Indians
to dispose of some old stock which they had been
unable to sell during the war. He arrived sometime
in May 1816, and erected a house not far from the
spot where later the American Fur Company took

22.   *Mich. Hist. Colls.*, XXX, 186.
23.   The Chapman *Hist. of Saginaw Co.*, 165.
24.   *Ibid*.
25.   *Ibid; Mich. Hist. Colls.*, VI, 427.
26.   *Mich. Hist. Colls.*, VIII, 244.

up their headquarters.[27] When Réaume came to assume the management of the company's business he and Campau soon disagreed. The hatred between them became stronger every day and the Indians began to take sides. At the forks of Tittabawassee, a store had been erected by the company, and Réaume had placed De Quindre, a young clerk, in charge of it. One day while he and his assistant were absent, the Indians, unquestionably incited by the opposition, entered the store. Soon brandy and provisions were appropriated, and the Indians feasted and made merry until the owners returned. A drunken Indian was a dangerous foe to handle, especially when hostile and bent on doing all the harm possible, so De Quindre could do nothing and Réaume was forced to abandon this little outpost at the Forks. Moreover, such a close boycott was maintained at Saginaw by the opposition, that he was unable to do any trading.[28]

The Abbott Brothers, fur dealers at Detroit, represented the American Fur Company at that post, and James Abbott was their superintendent for this district.[29] He removed Réaume and, in 1828, appointed Ephraim and Gordon Williams as his successors.[30]

Meanwhile Louis Campau had left for the Grand River Valley and Antoine Campau had charge of his old post; nevertheless the bitter feud which had formerly existed still smouldered among the Indians. But the Forks, from which the opposition had succeeded

27. The Chapman *Hist. of Saginaw Co.*, 158; *Mich. Hist. Colls.*, IV, 288; VII, 263.
28. *Mich. Hist. Colls.*, VIII, 244.
29. *Ibid*, I, 24; VIII, 244.
30. *Ibid*, VIII, 244.

in driving away De Quindre, was too good a business point to leave unoccupied and they felt that the interests of their firm demanded that some efforts be made to re-establish trading relations in that vicinity, and not abandon such a lucrative spot to the enemy. Courage and tact were needed, because not only was the savage hostile, defiant, and insolent, but in this contest the traders had become accustomed to ill-treat and abuse their Indian allies to hold them in subordination. The Williams Brothers forbade any such ill-treatment on penalty of dismissal and proceeded to station their clerks at the contested spot and transport their goods thither. Their endeavors were crowned with success. In spite of all opposition they were able to hold their own and secure considerable trade for their company.[31]

Outposts were also established in other regions, one at River Au Sable, one on the Cass, and one at Sebawaing. Several Indian women were commissioned to trade for them, and Joseph Trombley, a man known to be very shrewd at making a bargain, was sent to establish a post in Bay County.[32] The two brothers were far from idle. Many trips were made to Thunder Bay to collect furs and their sloop the *Savage* was constantly carrying Indian goods and peltries from Saginaw to Detroit.

E. S. Williams relates that during the first winter, they put up five packs of muskrat, containing 2,500 skins. Twelve years later the number had increased to 28,000. Likewise, the first year brought them from four to five hundred marten skins, and these increased

31. *Ibid*, 244-5.
32. *Ibid*, II, 316-18.

annually until the number reached from 1,500 to 2,000.[33]

The "Shiawassee Exchange," sometimes known as the "Williams Exchange," was a well-known trading station in these regions. This was established bv B. O. and A. L. Williams. In 1829 they came from Pontiac, Oakland County, to explore the region. Two years later they took up a permanent residence there and continued to trade until 1837, when the post was abandoned.[34] Their field for collecting furs comprised Oakland, Livingston, Ingham, Eaton, Clinton, Shiawassee, Genesee, Lapeer, parts of Tuscola, Saginaw, and Gratiot counties, while the Chippeway and the Saginaw tribes were their chief customers.[35]

Other hunters and trappers, known to have traversed the Saginaw section and to have pitched their trading camps there for longer or shorter periods were Louis Branford, known as the peacemaker in the trader's circle; Leon Suay, the Frenchman who is said to have deserted the upper circles of society for the hunter's career, hence considered himself in the better class of French traders; old Baptiste Desnoyers, Henry Connor, Richard Godfroy, and Whitmore Knaggs.[36] There were many others, but to describe each little post or outpost with its founder would be unnecessary. Suffice it to say that they were found in every spot in these regions that was favorable for trade.

Naturally, the principal trading-marts were located

33. For the trading career of E. and G. Williams see *Mich. Hist. Colls.*, III, 602; IV, 376, 475; VII, 239-40; VIII, 233-59.
34. *Mich. Hist. Colls.*, XXXII, 253.
35. *Ibid*, XI, 243-7; XXX, 345-6, 355, 377; XXXII, 253.
36. The Chapman *Hist. of Saginaw Co.*, 127, 160-3; *Mich. Hist. Colls.*, XXXII, 251.

in the great river valleys, yet there were many minor posts scattered throughout Michigan; there was the old French trader Micheau in Oakland County.[37] Austin in Kalamazoo;[38] the old bachelor John Parish in Mecosta,[39] and John Baptiste Barboux and A. B. Goodwin in Jackson.[40] Chappee, now in the employ of the American Fur Company, still continued to meet and barter with the Menominee Indians; but one day when he returned from the woods he found his hut occupied and all his possessions removed. William Farnsworth and Charles Brush had come to settle in this region; here was a nice hut in the wilderness all ready to receive them. Farnsworth easily induced the red man to grant him the land where Chappee's hut was located and immediately took up his abode in the latter. Possession was the whole law on that rude frontier, so Chappee did not stop to question his right but piled his belongings into his canoe and sailed to the foot of Chappee Rapids where he pitched his camp.[41]

Thus briefly have been indicated some of the men and forces at work in the river valleys and interior regions of Michigan under the American régime. Her army of traders, designated Yankees, numbered in their midst Englishmen, Scotchmen, Frenchmen, and half-breeds. On the whole they lived in peace and on friendly terms with their dusky allies of the woods, and fewer murders of traders are noted than in previous régimes. Old traders like Robinson, fearlessly tramped the woods alone unmolested by the Indians,

37. *Mich. Hist. Colls.*, VII, 557.
38. *Ibid*, X, 58.
39. *Ibid*, XXX, 27.
40. *Hist. of Jackson Co.* (Ed. Interstate Pub. Co.), 896, 959.
41. *Mich. Hist. Colls.*, I, 264-5.

and the story goes that in later years the grounds of Campau's home at Grand Rapids were a favorite gathering place for the older Indians, who liked to meet and recall the good old trading days of former years.[42] This happier relation was, no doubt, largely due to the greater kindness and tact used by the American peltry dealer in his treatment of the red men. Intending as he did to make his post a permanent abode, he could not afford to arouse the savage hatred of those around him, as did the early French rovers who tarried but a short time in any one place.

Alien influence was no longer present to lure away this fickle forest being, or incite him to fall upon helpless men in their frontier posts. Then, too, it must be kept in mind that the contact of savagery and civilization for over a century and a half had subdued and modified the former, so that though the Indian had not learned to love his pale-face companion, he had at least learned to depend upon and tolerate him.

And now to return to the old entrepots of trade; posts like Michilimackinac, Detroit, and Sault Ste. Marie, all of which had played prominent parts in Michigan's forest commerce from its infancy.

The American Fur Company used Sault Ste. Marie as a depot of trade and, immediately after the War of 1812, placed the post under the management of John Johnston. He was allowed $40,000 annually to expend for Indian goods, salaries of clerks and other expenses.[43] This post, the first prominent trading-

---

42. Richmond, *Fur Traders of Grand River Valley*, 39-44.
43. Memoir of John Johnston, in *Mich. Hist. Colls.*, XXXVI, 73-4. He, however, took charge of the post only for the years 1816 and 1817.

mart of Michigan, which had been twice abandoned and again established, became once more a rendezvous where traders gathered to obtain their outfits, and some of the old-time feasting, drinking, and revelry became a part of its life. According to William Johnston, as late as 1833 there was no market beyond the Sault on this lake highway from whence the western trader could supply his wants.[44]

The St. Joseph Valley remained a favorite region for peltry traders. The American Fur Company had its establishment there with its Indian interpreter, traders, and boatmen,[45] while many independents came,—some to make this valley a permanent home; others only to stay until they had secured a few packs of fur for the market.

As the American Fur Company was the dominating force at Michilimackinac during the American régime, so the individual trader was the power in Detroit. In 1820 from eight to ten firms located there were directly or indirectly engaged in the Indian trade. While the company, usually, hired their men to go into the fields, Detroit and other places followed the old custom of furnishing the merchandise, with which traders sought the Indian country, and in the opening

---

44. Johnston's Letters on the Fur Trade, in *Mich. Hist. Colls.*, XXXVII, 143.
45. List of Employees, from Account Book for 1818-19, in *Wis. Hist. Colls.*, XII, 159. Only one employee is here listed for St. Joseph and the Wabash, but as others are given as for "Wabash, &c" it is thought that it means "and St. Joseph," and that the latter is left out merely for brevity's sake. In the "invoice outward" for 1821-2, Joseph Bertrand is given an outfit for St. Joseph and dependencies, Aug. 22, 1821, and the following year outfits are furnished Joseph Bertrand and Pièrre Navarre. *Wis. Hist. Colls.*, XI, 376.

of the spring returned with the proceeds of their sale.[46]
Many Detroit firms were most extensively engaged in
this trade. It is said that the Abbott Brothers alone
at one time had as many as seven establishments
there.[47]

The fur trade was still the one great occupation of
the day. A rough estimate places the amount of
furs collected and sent from this post in the summer
of 1822 alone as worth $300,000.[48] "It must be
allowed," says a writer in the Detroit *Gazette*, "that
the amount of fur collected annually and sold by the
traders and inhabitants is considerable in our list of
articles for transportation, indeed, it is almost the
only article worth note. How much more consoling
it would be could we feel that even a small portion of
our fur could return to our territory in cash to be
expended in erecting mills.... Instead all furs which
are collected by our merchants go as toward payments of debts contracted for foreign fabrics or in exchange for them, not only the fur but the money
received for them." [49]

So extensive were the operations of the American
Fur Company located at Michilimackinac during this
régime, that the little trade done by other firms and
traders at that place was thrown more or less in the
shadow. Robert Stuart managed the company's affairs
during these most flourishing years of the American
Fur Company, as well as the Michigan trade.[50] When
Astor sold out his interests and retired from business

46. Detroit *Gazette*, Dec. 15, 1820.
47. *Ibid*, Dec. 22, 1820.
48. *Ibid*, Jan. 4, 1822.
49. *Ibid*, Jan. 4, 1822.
50. Bingham, *Mich. Biographies*, 621-2.

in 1834, the great corporation dissolved. Crooks headed a company which bought out the northern department on the Great Lakes, retaining Michili-mackinac as its headquarters, while the western department was operated from St. Louis by another firm. The Crooks company retained the old name, but the great days of the American Fur Company were over, as were those of the Michigan fur trade.[51]   The great army of fur traders, all intent on one occupation, the capturing and killing of the furred creatures of her forests, were fully exhausting the source of supply on the hunting grounds, so that the last days of Michigan's forest commerce was fast approaching.

51. *Atlantic Monthly*, CIII, 532.

19

CHAPTER IX

THE CLOSING DAYS OF THE MICHIGAN FUR TRADE

IN the latter part of the 1830's the Michigan fur trade began to decline, and men who for years had plied their canoes on her rivers and tramped the trails of her forests in search of pelts were seeking new fields of labor.[1]

Long ago the United States factory system for Indian trade had disappeared and it had been clearly proved that the government regulation of the fur business was a decided failure.[2] Naturally, it found in men like Ramsay Crooks strong opponents. He called it a species of monopoly "of no real benefit to our tawny neighbors, and bemeaning to the Government," "and," said he, "those very Tribes who experienced in the greatest degree this fostering care of the Executive were the first to raise the Tomahawk against the American Settlements."[3] "Experience," said a writer in the Detroit *Gazette*, "is considered as decidedly against the government taking any part in the Indian trade."[4] This opinion was prevalent among Indians and traders alike. Hence it is not surprising that the Government closed its factory doors in 1822, and thus put an end to a system adopted with the best

1. Thus Rix Robinson gave up the Indian trade in 1837, and Martin Ryerson in 1839, etc.
2. *U. S. Statutes at Large*, III, 679, Chap. 54.
3. Letter of Ramsay Crooks in *Wis. Hist. Colls.*, XIX, 349-350.
4. Detroit *Gazette*, April 26, 1822; see also *Ibid*, April 12, 1822 and Jan. 17, 1822.

of intentions for the red man's welfare, but wholly impracticable under the existing conditions.

Various factors contributed to its failure. Indian agents furnished merchandise of poor quality. This was bad policy, for the red man was no longer to be fooled, and contemptuously ever afterward called all inferior goods American. Moreover, the British and even the French had been accustomed to grant them goods outright as gifts, while these new people demanded pay. The government officials were salaried men, hence lacked the energy and hustle of the trader, who clearly saw that the fruit of his labor was his own, so that the harder he worked the bigger would be his reward. The former were men often unacquainted with the western forests and its commerce; the latter were skilled traffickers in the western woods who knew every trick of the trade. The former remained at their posts, strangers to their customers; the latter sought the Indian on his hunting ground and pulled every available wire for trade, furnishing him goods on credit and as much liquor as possible, seeking out and making friends of the influential chiefs, and marrying into their families. With such a difference in the men at work and the methods used, it is no wonder that the latter succeeded where the former failed.[5]

As the factory system had its enemies, so also did the license system, but unlike the former it continued in operation during the entire Michigan fur régime. The hostility raised up against it[6] was largely due to

5. *Amer. State Papers* (Indian Affairs), II, 202-7; Wis. Hist. Society *Proceedings*, 1889, 85n.
6. *Mich. Hist. Colls.*, XIX, 17; *Wis. Hist. Colls.*, XIX, 459; Crooks' letter-book, 117, 108.

certain abuses which had crept in; for instance, Major Puthuff, the Indian agent at Michilimackinac, is said to have reaped a rich harvest from these licenses. Originally two dollars each were charged for them, no doubt to cover expenses.   Puthuff charged fifty dollars each, on the plea that by so doing he might reduce applications for them.   Thus, according to Mathew Irwin, he got a nice little sum of seven thousand dollars in a single year.[7]

It had been the policy of French and English fur traders to discourage all settlements, as settlements meant the destruction of the fur trade.   Government officials and others who profited thereby joined the trader in his opposition.   This was clearly shown in their hostility to Cadillac's scheme of forming a colony at Detroit, as well as in the statement of the English Lord Commissioners when they said: "Let the savages enjoy their deserts in quiet.   Were they driven from their forests the peltry trade would decrease."[8]   Leach declared that it was for the interest of those carrying freight and passengers on the Great Lakes to decry Michigan lands and eulogize Illinois and Wisconsin; so that as late as 1859 Horace Greeley, in the New York *Tribune*, spoke of the Northern Peninsula, as "cold and uninviting to the cultivator, diversified by vast swamps, sterile, gravelly knolls, and dense forests."[9]   This attitude of the lake traffickers, with

7.   Indian letter-book, in *Wis. Hist. Colls.*, XIX, 459, 481-2. It seems that $3,200 were received from Bartlett for issuing licenses to their agents, and $4,000 from others. Major Puthuff had been made Indian agent at Michilimackinac in July 1817.   *Mich. Hist. Colls.*, XIX, 404.

8.   Sparks, *Franklin*, IV, 318; see Hansard, *Parl. Debates*, XXII, 382, 409.

9.   Leach, *Hist. of Grand Traverse Region*, 50.

the constant tendency of the peltry dealer to pursue a course of deception and misrepresentation as to the actual conditions in the interior, was doubtless partly responsible for the fact that emigrants were slow to penetrate into her wilderness and make it their permanent abode; as late as 1810, the population was estimated at only 4,783, and all commerce was even at that late date confined to fur trade and to carrying a few supplies for the garrison located at Detroit.[10] Then too it must be kept in mind that British influence within Michigan was strong long after British official occupation had ceased.

But if the French and the English had discouraged settlement, the Yankee made no effort in that direction; rather, he put forth every effort to persuade the red men to give up their hunting grounds.[11] The War of 1812 had brought a change of spirit, because during the struggle men had penetrated into the wilds of this region and had come to realize that the interior was not as bad as had been depicted. This changed attitude is clearly shown in an editorial printed in the Detroit *Gazette* of January, 1822. After eulogizing the settler and stating his purpose, it continues: "Compared with these objects, the advantages to be reaped from the fur trade dwindle to nothing. Surely, it is of more consequence to a nation that a wilderness and solitary place should be cultivated, than that it should be permitted to remain in a state of nature."[12]

10. Detroit *Gazette*, June 7, 1822.
11. Louis Campau assisted Gov. Cass in making a treaty with the Indians; Whitmore Knaggs, the Detroit treaty, also the Saginaw and Chicago treaties; Kinzie and Hubbard, the Chicago treaty of 1833. Robinson assisted in adjusting many relations with the Indians.
12. Detroit *Gazette*, Jan. 18, 1822.

But there was one obstacle in the way of transform-
ing this wilderness into cultivated fields, and that was
its original owner, the Indian. He claimed as his
property the hunting ground which the Yankee trader
had almost despoiled of its wild animals. It was here
that the influence of the old trader upon the Indian
was brought into service, who was largely instrumental
in inducing the latter to cede large tracts of land to
the Government.[13]   In 1807 the region around Detroit
was turned over to the United States, with the stipulation that as long as it remained government property
the savage should have the privilege of hunting and
fishing there.[14]

The Saginaw treaty of 1819[15] gave another portion
of eastern Michigan. Then followed the treaty of
Sault Ste. Marie in 1820,[16] the two Chicago treaties
in 1821[17] and 1833,[18] and the Washington treaty in
1836;[19] until, finally, by the treaty of La Pointe in
1842,[20] the last strip of Indian land in Michigan passed
into the hands of the United States Government.
Government possession meant the influx of settlers,
and the influx of settlers meant the death blow to the
Indian fur trade.

As settlers began to enter, the question of regulating
the liquor traffic became more complicated. To be
sure, it had been a troublesome problem during the
entire period. Just as in the French and English

13. See note 11.
14. *U. S. Statutes* (Indian Treaties), 105-7.
15. *Ibid*, 203-5.
16. *Ibid*, 206-7.
17. *Ibid*, 218-21.
18. *Ibid*, 442-6.
19. *Ibid*, 491-95.
20. *Ibid*, 591-3.

régime the government decrees against it had been evaded, so they were practically a dead letter in this period. Large quantities of liquor were smuggled in,[21] because traders felt that it was, as Robert Stuart called it, a "sheer necessity" as long as traders of the Hudson Bay Company were carrying barrels of it with them on the frontier.[22]

The licenses granted traders stipulated that if any liquor was furnished to the Indian without special authority, the latter might confiscate the goods as well as any liquor kept on hand by the traders.[23] William Burnett relates a story, showing how the Indians took the Government at its word. The sloop *General Hunter* arrived at St. Joseph loaded with goods, part of which were the property of a Mr. Pattison of that place, and part belonged to Mr. Kinzie of Chicago. As Pattison was in Detroit, one Chadonet promised to take charge of his goods. Another boat loaded with barrels anchored, and Chadonet on inquiry was told that they contained liquor. He remonstrated, since liquor was forbidden and was liable to be seized by the Indians. The captain, however, refused to carry it back, hence it was landed. The Potawatomi Indians who had witnessed the performance kept close watch of the barrels. When later an attempt was made by the owners to remove the liquor the Potawatomis dutifully carried out the orders of the Government and seized the goods, illegally brought into their midst.[24]

---

21. Chittenden, *Fur Trade of the Far West*, I, 26, 29, 31; Crooks, letter-books, p. 27.
22. *Mich. Hist. Colls.*, XXXVII, 236-7.
23. *Burton Hist. Colls.*, MS. Vol. CXV, 37.
24. *Ibid.* Sibley Papers.

But if it had been a problem to enforce liquor laws in the early régime, it became doubly so when the settlers' shacks began to dot the wilderness; for the liquor law extended only to the red man's country and did not affect regions where the Indian title to land had been extinguished. If then the red-skin could not get his drinks from the pale-face trader, he could visit the hut of the emigrant, who was bound neither by license stipulation nor by laws of the Indian country, and usually he was there supplied with all he desired.[25]

The decline in the fur trade was apparently felt sooner at Detroit than farther inland in Michigan. Already in 1827, before some of the interior trading posts had yet been established, Astor wrote to Crooks that he contemplated sending Clupp to Detroit to see what could be done about closing up the business at that place.[26] This did not meet the approval of Crooks. He held that to abandon Detroit altogether would leave the field open to their opponents who would lose no time in trying to hamper and annoy their northern department, particularly in Chicago. He advised Astor, at least, to keep an agent there to hold the enemy in check. That was all he could do. There

---

25. Detroit *Gazette*, Dec. 22, 1820. John Askin, Jr. writing to his father in 1807 speaks of the Ottawas at L'Arbre Croche not drinking liquor. "Whiskey & rum," he says, "is a drug. The Indians do not purchase one gallon per month. I saw upwards of 60 of them at one time together. Spirits, rum, & whiskey was offered for nothing to them if they would drink but they refused it with disdain." Thwaites says that Shawnee, brother of Tecumseh, in 1805 assumed the character of a prophet and began religious instructions among the Indians. Among parts of the new doctrine was abjuration of the white man's fire-water. *Wis. Hist. Colls.*, XIX, 322-3.
26. Crooks' letter-book, 294-5.

was no hope of making any money in the fur trade at that post much longer.[27]

Astor's retirement from the fur trade and Ramsay Crooks' purchase of the northern department have already been noted. In 1854, the American Fur Company was bought out by J. B. Hubbel of St. Paul and all its effects at Michilimackinac were removed.[28] This was the final blow to the Michigan fur trade. Long before this a large number of the interior posts had been abandoned, and the men who had been prominent figures in this frontier commerce had either wandered westward with the Indians, died, or sought other fields of labor. The removal of the company from Michilimackinac meant not only the destruction of this latter post as a great entrepot of trade, but it meant the fall of numerous interior posts not already abandoned. It meant, practically, that Michigan fur trading days were over. While in 1840 the census reports[29] record a sale of $54,232 worth of fur, in 1850 no sales are mentioned, and only thirty-three men are listed as fur traders.[30] The trading régime had passed away and the roving trader had resigned his place to the tiller of the soil.

27. *Ibid*, 304-6.
28. *Atlantic Monthly*, CIII, 532.
29. *U. S. Census Report* 1840. See map in appendix for the amount of fur and its distribution at this date.
30. *Ibid*, 1850.

CHAPTER X

The Trader's Life

NO history of the fur trade is complete without giving a glimpse of the life of the men engaged in it. To most of us who have been introduced to these pioneer scouts through stories of adventure, the words "fur trade" and "fur trader" call forth a mental picture of a wild, free life, full of romance and fascinating peril. But a closer study will reveal that to the actual participant, particularly in the early trade, it was a life of many hardships, at times seemingly barren of all pleasures. One thing is certain, there must have been something besides greed for the almighty dollar in the shape of a beaver-pelt, that enticed men into the wilderness in spite of untold suffering, so that according to Du Chesneau, there was not a family of any condition and quality whatever that did not have children, brothers, uncles, or nephews among the hunters of the West.[1] This life, free from bonds of civilized society, full of dangerous hunting exploits, and narrow escapes from the Indian scalping-knife and starvation, held a certain fascination for these folk, which made them unwilling to return to civilized realms when once they had got a taste of it. So the writer's aim is not to detract one iota from the romance of this life, if such romance is there, but simply to portray it as far as possible as it really was.

The daily life of these men, their food and dress,

---

1. *N. Y. Col. Docs.*, IX, 140, 152.

their hardships and recreation, their methods of trade, their character, and relation to the Indian were interesting. At first, when few traders were in the field, the class could be roughly divided into two divisions; the coureurs de bois, that unlicensed, lawless trader of the woods, and the licensed trader. Later, as the number of men engaged in this commerce increased, distinct classes arose, such as the bourgeois, the voyageur, the mangeurs-de-lard, the clerks, engagés, hivernans or winterers. Besides these the large fur-trading companies employed many artisans at their posts.

The terms "licensed trader" and "coureur de bois" scarcely need explanation. The latter are the picturesque figures of the pioneer fur trade. Mostly they were French or half-breeds, who believed that the furred creatures of the forest were the monoply of neither king nor company, but the spoils of all, and hence they defied all law to the contrary. They plunged into the wilderness to barter with the savage, adopted his customs and his life, and married his daughters. Men who could ply paddle, hunt, trap, and speak the Indian tongue almost as well as the savage himself; gay, lighthearted, care-free, capable of great endurance, a strange mixture of civilization and savagery, with a predominance of the latter,— such were the rovers of the wood, the coureurs de bois of the fur-trading régime.[2]

In the latter days when the system of trade became more organized there were other classes to be reckoned with. There was the "bourgeois" at the head of the

---

2. For the coureurs de bois, see *N. Y. Col. Docs.*, IX, 152-154, 140-42, 131; Irving, *Astoria*, 18-21; La Hontan, *N. V. to N. A.*, index; Wis. Hist. Society *Proceedings*, 1889, 66-67; Parkman, *Old Régime*, 313-15.

trade, the commander-in-chief, the supreme sovereign
at the permanent post, who ruled his little army of
traders in a sort of military fashion. His was the
business to plan for the subsistence of the men, to
drum up trade, to send out trading expeditions to
various sections, to see that furs were properly packed
and shipped away, to keep in touch with his representatives in various sections,—a man of manifold duties
and great responsibilities.

The man who was sent out with trading expeditions
and was king of the temporary rendezvous was called
the "partisan", and his duties were similar to those
of the bourgeois.[3]

An interesting and picturesque figure in the trading
world was the "voyageur", whose life, as his name
implies, was largely spent upon the water, the lakes,
and inland rivers, though not wholly confined thereto.
Usually he was a man of powerful physique, of a rough,
coarse exterior, wholly illiterate, and often extremely
cowardly. He has been called the slave of the fur
trade, for his labors were extremely heavy and he often
suffered from lack of food; yet the French voyageur
of our Great Lakes is said to have endured all with the
patience of a Job, and in spite of prodigious labor and
much suffering he often made the air resound with some
simple Canadian boat-song like the following:[4]

> "Dans mon chemin, j'ai rencontré
> Trois cavalières, bien montées;
> L'on, ton, laridon danée
> L'on, ton, laridon, dai.

3. Chittenden, *Fur Trade of the Far West*, I, 51-2.
4. *Mich. Hist. Colls.*, I, 359, 365-8; III, 14; XXX, 140-4, 613; Chittenden, *Fur Trade of the Far West*, I. 55-57.

Trois cavalières, bien montées,
L'une à cheval, l'autre à pied;
L'on, ton, laridon danée
L'on, ton, laridon, dai.[5]

The "mangeurs de lard" or pork-eaters were those delicate fellows who dined on the flesh of animals and were not yet inured to the hardier fare of bear's grease, lard, and lyed-corn, the stock food of the ordinary trader. These were the raw recruits, the greenhorns, the tenderfeet of the trade, who, not partaking of the ordinary food of the trader, was unable to endure the physical exertion of the old hand. They usually performed the more menial services and hired out for such low wages that they were unable to keep out of debt, hence were forced to stay in their employer's service,—though many of them would, no doubt, have gladly deserted.[6]

The clerk stood next to the bourgeois in responsibility and in the trader's social circle. Often in the latter's absence he succeeded to his authority and his duties. He frequently commanded posts and was a most trusted servant of the company of which he sometimes was a shareholder, but more often a salaried man.[7]

---

5. Another boat song began

La jeune Sophie
Chantait l'autre jour,
Son echo lui repete,
Que non pas d'amour
N'est pas de bon jour

Je suis jeune et belle,
Je vieux mé engagé
Un amant fidele
Je suis Jeune, etc.

Mich. Hist. Colls., I, 366-67.
6. Johnston's letters on the fur trade, in *Mich. Hist. Colls.*, XXXVII, 168; Chittenden, *Fur Trade of the Far West*, I, 58.
7. Chittenden, *Fur Trade of the Far West*, I, 53.

The "hivernans", or winterers, were the men who spent several winters in the Indian country, hence were old hands at the trade.[8]   The common hired men of the company were sometimes termed engagés. Usually they were the boatmen.[9]   Then every large company which carried on the trade on an extensive scale was forced to keep on hand a large class of artisans, men skilled in various lines such as boat building, and the blacksmith's and carpenter's trades.[10] These were not only kept at the main post but were sent to all the various outposts of the company.   In the list of employees of the American Fur Company the following are noted as sent out from Michilimackinac to various posts: boatmen, masons, tailors, carpenters, interpreters, clerks, traders, and hunters.[11]

The free trapper, or independent hunter, was an important personage during the entire fur-trading régime.   He allied himself with no company, but was his own master, going where he pleased and doing what he pleased, and the entire fruit of his labors was his own. Sometimes several of these men were together for protection, but often each went alone, sought some Indian village, took up his abode, married an Indian maid, and there with his squaw and halfbreed children spent the greater part of the year, only once in a while coming in touch with the civilized world, when he brought his peltries to market.[12]

These were some of the classes of men who partici-

8. *Ibid*, I, 58; Wis. Hist. Society *Proceedings*, 1889, 79.
9. Wis. Hist. Society *Proceedings*, 1889, 77.
10. Chittenden, *Fur Trade of the Far West*, I, 57-58.
11. List of employees in A. F. Co's. account books, in *Wis. Hist. Colls.*, XII, 154-69.
12. Chittenden, *Fur Trade of the Far West*, I, 55.

pated in this forest commerce. That all were not fitted for its pursuit is evident. It demanded a powerful physique to cope with the hardships to be encountered. This was particularly true of the men out in the field searching for furs, or the voyageurs on the lakes or inland rivers transporting the merchandise or the product of the hunt. When the American Fur Company under Robert Stuart at Michilimackinac organized and systematized trade of that section, they sent to Montreal for a number of employees, voyageurs and clerks. A physical examination was demanded, as all weaklings were to be weeded out of service; for in this strenuous life only the fittest could survive. The old experienced trader was sought and every effort made to secure the men skilled in this vocation. The tenderfoot was out of place in this world.[13]

Fur traders have been described as ruffians of the coarsest stamp.[14] "Fierce, bold, and truculent as the Indian," says Parkman;[15] while Major Bassett calls them "the outcasts of all nations and the refuse of all mankind,"[16] men who vied with each other in cheating, plundering, and cursing the savage. Dablon relates how the French, whom we usually think of as the friendly fur trader in his relation to the Indians, ill-treated them, pillaging and carrying away their merchandise, and heaping upon them insolence and indignities.[17] Father Carheil paints a vivid picture of the life of lawlessness, drunkenness, debauchery,

13. *Mich. Hist. Colls.*, XI, 343-5.
14. Parkman, *Conspiracy of Pontiac*, 155.
15. *Ibid*, 137.
16. Ross and Catlin, *Landmarks of Wayne County and Detroit*, 198-9; *Mich. Hist. Colls.*, XXIX, 89-90, 106, 297.
17. *Jes. Rel.*, LIV, 197, 225.

and vice of the traders at Michilimaçkinac, and other Jesuits give similar pictures of conditions elsewhere; they were men as a rule, illiterate, who seemed to have no other purpose in life but to roam the forest and secure a few peltries.[18]   That they were not all of this type is certain.   Men like William Burnett of St. Joseph, Rix Robinson and the Campaus of the Grand River Valley, and John Johnston of the Sault, as well as many others, were intelligent and educated men, who had entered upon the trade and found in it a certain fascination in the shape of rich returns in cash, as well as something in the very nature of the occupation itself, which gave them no desire to return to regions where rules of etiquette and social ceremony held sway.[19]

To be sure, they cheated the Indian,—even the best of the traders,—for therein lay the enormous profit of the early fur trade.   The Indian sold the most valuable fur for a "mere whistle," some gew-gaw to adorn his vain person, or a drink to feed the "inner man."   But he at first did not know that he was cheated and was satisfied in his new possession, so it mattered little.

It is true, the Indian was often ill-treated by the trader.   Ephraim Williams tells how, when first he and his brother came to Saginaw to trade, they were forced to stipulate in the articles of agreement with their men, that any ill-treatment of the Indian would be followed by instant dismissal, for ill conduct had been steadily increasing among the men there.[20]   And

18.   *Ibid*, LXV, 189-253; XXII, 241-3; LXIII, 133-5, etc.
19.   Wis. Hist. Soc. *Proceedings*, 1889, 92.
20.   *Mich. Hist. Colls.*, VIII, 244.   He says the traders had become savage toward the Indian for little or no cause.

it is not at all surprising that such treatment was meted out to the savage when we consider how the traders treated one another. Bitter feuds existed among the opposition men; each used any means at hand to down the other fellow,—blackmailing, boycotting, even murder.[21] On the other hand, there is much testimony as to the most friendly relations existing between Indian and white traders. A large number married Indian women[22] and were content to spend their days in the Indian communities. By their kindness to the savage they opened up the way for the future settler and made the latter's entrance into the community a possibility. They helped to tame the Indian and make him dependent upon the white man,—often by harshness and firearms, it is true, but also by kindness. The traders' services were often used in influencing him to give up his hunting ground to the emigrant and peacefully vacate lands which he rightly considered his, to a race which he felt had often cheated and ill-treated him.[23] That the coarse, lawless ruffians who would stop at nothing to gain their ends were present in the majority, there is no question, but these very men, with all their lawlessness, and coarseness, "outcasts and refuse of mankind," were making civilized society in these sections possible and by their influence saved many a future infant colony from the tomahawk and the scalping-knife.[24]

21. For example see p. 138.
22. Many of the traders in Michigan had Indian wives, John Johnston at Sault Ste. Marie, William Burnett, Rix Robinson, Edward Biddle, John Drew, and many others.
23. See note 11, Chapter IX.
24. For the importance of the forerunners and scouts, see Wis. Hist. Society *Proceedings*, 1889, 53, 82, 90, 97-8.

Their life, seemingly stripped of every comfort in the shape of food, clothing, and recreation, is a fitting excuse for their character. Food, in which at best there was little variety, was often wanting. It was mostly lyed-corn and wild rice; bread was a luxury never thought of.[25] Alexander Henry tells how this corn was prepared. It was boiled in strong lye, then the husk was removed, and it was washed and dried. In that state it was soft and friable like rice.[26] A bushel of corn and two pounds of fat was a month's allowance, as a trader was not supposed to consume more than one-fourth of corn and one-half pint of bear's grease, oil, or fat at a meal.[27] At times they were forced to live on the wild rice when their food gave out, and many times they were brought to the verge of starvation if lost, or if they failed to find an Indian camp as they had expected.[28] The story told by Le Jeune of the hardships endured by early missionaries among the Indians no doubt is also a fairly good picture of what the trader many times endured.[29] Perrault relates how he was forced to lend three fawn-skins of rice to a neighbor who was reduced to eating moss from the pines,[30] while Henry came upon a man-eater near Sault Ste. Marie. Provisions had given out because the fishery there, on which both Indians and traders depended so much, had failed, hence this sole surviver of a no doubt desperate band of traders had been

25. *Mich. Hist. Colls.*, I, 365-6, XXXVII, 138; Henry, *Travels and Adventures*, 52-3; Mackenzie, *Voyages*, I, xlvii.
26. Henry, *Travels and Adventures*, 52-3.
27. *Ibid.*
28. Perrault's Narrative, in *Mich. Hist. Colls.*, XXXVII, 523-4.
29. See Chapter I.
30. Perrault's Narrative, in *Mich. Hist. Colls.*, XXXVII, 563.

forced to feed upon his dead companions.[31]   This was
one of the dark, ugly, desperate sides of the trader's
life, which threw the romance of the whole into shadow.
Under the open sky, with the green-sward for a table-
cloth and the nearby stream for a finger bowl, they
sat down day after day, meal after meal, to dine all
by themselves, devouring the corn and fat allotted
for each meal.   If Chittenden's story is true, they had
as healthy an appetite as any normal man; for, he
says, "The Canadians, despite the scantiness of their
allowance of food, were great eaters, when they could
get what they wanted, and it was a common saying in
the fur business that two would devour off-hand the
whole side of a buffalo."[32]

At night these men camped by some rivulet or
spring. Wrapping themselves in a blanket with gun
near at hand, they often lay down upon the bare
ground, or perhaps with a few green boughs for a bed,—
a coat, saddle, pack of fur, or a little greasy pillow
under their heads,—a restless rest, no doubt, since
they were in constant danger of being attacked by
wild beasts of the forest or the savage Indian.[33]

As to recreation and diversions, to civilized man it
must seem that there were none, that their life was
the very embodiment of monotony and humdrum;
the same food meal after meal; the same pursuit,
traversing miles and miles, sometimes on horseback;
more often on foot, over swamps and through almost
impenetrable forest; the same company day after day.
One trader thus describes his daily routine: "I rise

31.   Henry, *Travels and Adventures*, 207.
32.   Chittenden, *Fur Trade in the Far West*, I, 57 n.
33.   *Mich. Hist. Colls.*, I, 366.

with the sun. I go to see my traps. If some savages arrive, I trade for their peltries, then I eat some "tallibi" (kind of white-fish) three times a day. There you are. I find the time long and I fear my constitution is seriously affected by that kind of life, but what can you do?"[34] Topics of conversation were necessarily few, confined to the events of the hunting grounds. The lonely hunter who had not yet learned the tongue of the Indians among whom he had come was reduced to silence for days and even months.

Ephraim Williams tells of the Indian's love for telling stories and listening to those of traders. He would lie down, smoke, and tell stories, which were usually very long. He invented them as he went along. Naturally, many of them dealt with animal life and things concerning the hunt. One he mentions, showing the kind of stories thus told, was how the beaver came by his flat tail and the muskrat his round one.[35] To the one who had become intimate with the Indian tongue and Indian life, here was a break in the monotony of existence.

But a bigger break came into the humdrum of his life when after twelve or eighteen months in the woods he brought the product of his hunt to the larger trading centers like Sault Ste. Marie and Michilimackinac. There gathered at such times a motley crowd of a thousand or more from many parts of the wilderness. Indians with their feather-adorned heads, and hideous, painted, grinning faces were there, accompanied by their squaws and papooses; also coureurs de bois and voyageurs in their bright-hued flannel or calico shirts,

34. Masson, *Les Bourgeois*, I, 34.
35. *Mich. Hist. Colls.*, VIII, 253-4.

buckskin trousers, tasseled caps, cowhide shoes, or brightly colored moccasins; squaw-men with their Indian wives and troops of half-breed children; soldiers, clerks, commandants, and in earlier days black-robed priests; French, Scotch, English, and Yankee. The men from the wilderness brought their furs and sought in return a new supply of merchandise, some tobacco and liquor, some more tallow and corn, but above all they came to revel and feast to their heart's content. Eat, drink, and be merry, seemed their motto, for tomorrow comes again the call of the wild to leave these so-called halls of civilized life and go back to nature. So mid the yelping of dogs, the crying of children, the screeching of the fiddle, and the curses of men, they feasted and drank and danced, often as long as a single beaver pelt was left; for this, to many of them, was the only gleam of pleasure in their life,—their Christmas, New Year's, and Fourth of July in one; so they were anxious to make the most of the few days at their disposal before they were again to go back to another twelve or eighteen months of hardships and solitude.[36]

And now a word as to the method of trade. In early days it was based on credit, and this method was maintained in one place or another to the close of the régime. After obtaining his license the trader proceeded to his destination with his two canoes, each manned by six men and usually containing a thousand crowns worth of goods. The latter were as a rule obtained from Montreal merchants on credit;

36. La Hontan, *N. V. to N. A.*, I, 54; Irving, *Astoria*, 25-26; Mackenzie, *Voyages*, I, ii; *Margry, Déc. et étab.*, V, 85; Fowle, "Old Times in the Soo," *Evening News*, Feb. 22, 1913.

since the men who engaged in this commerce were not men of means, able to purchase the goods they wanted, but were indebted from year to year until they brought the return in furs. If the trade failed they were usually unable to pay. Ten thousand crowns worth of goods were in La Hontan's days rated at fifteen per cent more than could be obtained for them for ready money in the colony. This, he says, sometimes brought in a clear profit of seven hundred per cent,— sometimes more, sometimes less. The amount of goods in the canoes usually had a purchase power of as many beaver skins as would load four canoes, or about one hundred sixty packs of skins, forty skins in a pack, and counting each pack as worth fifty crowns the whole amounted to about eight thousand crowns. This profit was divided as follows: the merchant took six thousand crowns for the license and a thousand for the goods granted on credit; out of the six thousand four hundred crowns of the surplus he again deducted forty per cent, amounting to two thousand five hundred sixty crowns; and the rest was divided among the six men of each canoe; bringing them six hundred crowns apiece.[37]

The route taken by the early trader as already mentioned was the upper one. When a portage was reached the goods had to be taken out and carried by the men. Numerous were these stops, and with two, sometimes three, of these packages carried on their backs or suspended in slings from their foreheads, men trudged back and forth until the goods were unloaded and the canoes finally emptied and carried over. These packages weighed from eighty to ninety pounds;

37. La Hontan, *N. V. to'N. A.*, I, 100-101.

Masson says, from eighty to one hundred and twenty,[38] but they were seldom as heavy as the latter figure. Johnston in his account of Lake Superior describes the usual method of carrying goods over the portages. This was done by leather straps or thongs called tump-lines, the middle of which were broad and fitted to the forehead of the carrier. The first bale or piece was tied so as to lie a little above the reins, the second was lifted over the head and deposited without tying on the first. Thus loaded, the engagés trotted off to the places chosen for deposit, which in large portages were from two to three miles apart. This was repeated until the whole was transported, when they set off for the canoe, which was carried on the shoulders, and so they continued until night, only stopping once or twice to light a pipe or for a meal.[39]

The "pork eaters" were able to carry only one package and that with difficulty, as they could not keep it on their heads. "I never thought," says Johnston, "that men could undergo, and become so inured to hardships. To see some of them with two or three pieces, some .... carried six pieces, and see them rush and splash through the mud and water like so many wild cattle, is astonishing."[40]

The licensed trader on reaching his destination sought some Indian village whence he despatched his men to the various gathering places of the neighboring tribes. The independent trader and the coureurs de

---

38. Masson, *Les Bourgeois*, II, 165.
39. M. Johnston's account of Lake Superior in Masson, *Les Bourgeois*, II, 165; see also Johnston's letters on the fur trade, in *Mich. Hist..Colls.*, XXXVII, 168.
40. Johnston's letters on the fur trade, in *Mich. Hist. Colls.*, XXXVII, 168.

bois pushed into the wilderness alone, spending one, two, or three years among the Indians. A great number of the American Fur Company's employees were salaried, while some traders in Detroit and other places continued the old credit method of trade.[41]

Outfits, amounting to from four to five thousand dollars were carried into the wilderness by different men and in turn partitioned out among their men,[42] blankets, various colored cloths and strouds, beads, brooches, arm-bands, ear-bobs, wampum, shawls, handkerchiefs, ribbons, sleigh-bells, looking-glasses, combs, knives, scissors, shot, powder, guns, tobacco, liquor, and many other things that tickled the Indian's fancy.[43] From forty and fifty to three hundred dollars' worth were given out in credits to men who in turn went out and sought the Indian and granted him credit.[44] Just as the profit of the early voyageur's trade was largely absorbed by the Montreal merchant, so the Astor company usurped most of it during their régime. The factor was required to pay in advance eighty-one and one-half per cent on the cost of blankets, strouds, etc., to cover the cost of transportation from New York to Michilimackinac, and, if purchased in New York, fifteen and one-third per cent advance for transportation, and thirty-three and one-third per cent advance as profit on the whole amount.[45] The men in the employ of merchants and companies, then, could not grow rich on their trade, but several of the independent traders, like the lumber kings of the West,

41.   Detroit *Gazette*, Dec. 22, 1820.
42.   Wis. Hist. Society *Proceedings*, 1889, 86-89.
43.   See lists of goods bought by the Indian trader, in appendix.
44.   Wis. Hist. Society *Proceedings*, 1889, 89.
45.   *Senate Doc.*, No. 90, 22nd Cong., 1st Sess., II, 42.

amassed considerable fortunes.[46]   But this was practically the only business pursued in many sections in early days and, even when the Indian pushed further westward, many of the traders followed; and though many were forced to go into other occupations, yet they continued to deal in furs on a small scale until the end of their life.

Such then was the trader's life which had now come to a close within Michigan lands.   By the middle of the nineteenth century it was a thing of the past. To be sure, some trade was yet carried on by surviving hunters and trappers who loved the old days the best, but it was far from being the all-absorbing occupation it had been for over two centuries.   The Indians had given up their lands to the fast incoming settlers, and many of them, as well as the men who preferred the free life of a trader, had wandered to other hunting grounds.   The Yankee trader in his régime had pushed trade to the utmost, making no effort to preserve the furred animals for future harvest.   Hence the hunting grounds were despoiled.   Long before this the beaver had become scarce and many of the other wild animals followed fast on the decline.

From 1634 to 1850 the Michigan fur trade had passed under the control of three different nations, through three successive régimes.   The gay, affable, happy-go-lucky Frenchman blazed the trail.   He was the way-breaker, hence his period was the most romantic, filled with the greatest hardships.   His was a régime hampered and restricted by laws and decrees which were broken more often than kept, and wholly

46.   In Michigan, men like Robinson, the Campaus, etc., grew
        rich in the fur business.

ignored by the coureurs de bois, who pursued the beaver hunt with might and main, until the markets were overstocked and prices fell; his was a régime when black-robed priest and trader in pelts worked side by side; a period marked by the rise of a few large trading centers and many temporary rendezvous, maintained only as long as it suited the purpose of the roving coureur de bois.

Three important posts arose in this régime: Sault Ste. Marie, then Michilimackinac, and finally Detroit, the latter for some time usurping the trade of all the other posts. But Michilimackinac had too favorable a location to be consigned to oblivion for any length of time. She gradually regained her former place as a great entrepot of trade, a place she held until the end of the Michigan fur-trade régime. Besides the above named, posts had also been established in two other sections, the St. Joseph and the Grand River valleys.

But the English trader appeared and the rivalry between Frenchman and Briton became intense, the hostility bitter, for both wanted to have and keep control of this Eldorado in the western forest. The British trader paid a bigger price for furs and offered his merchandise for less. Moreover, he sought to entice the savage away with liquor and presents and to play upon his fear. But the French had won his friendship through intermarriage and the adoption of his mode of life, and besides he held the key positions for trade. Early the British and Dutch tried to get the trade of one of these key positions in Michigan, i. e., Michilimackinac, but were defeated.

The hostility between the two nations, largely intensified by this rivalry for furs, culminated in the

intercolonial wars which greatly hampered Michigan
trade, for they checked the means of transportation
and caused unrest among the Indians. French official
rule in Michigan came to an end at their close, but
the French trader remained for many years.

Three events prevented a rapid forward stride of
the British fur trade in Michigan. The first of these
was Pontiac's War which destroyed the posts at
Mackilimackinac and St. Joseph, and made Detroit
struggle desperately to hold her own, so that it was not
until 1765 that trade resumed its former proportions.
After that, trade flourished until it was again interfered with by the Revolutionary War, which aside
from the fact that it greatly hampered transportation,
affected trade less here, as the scene of war was in
other sections.

But another warfare greatly affected the fur commerce during this period. The free policy of trade
pursued by the British brought an influx of traders
who began to scheme and undersell each other, until
many were well-nigh ruined, and Michilimackinac
merchants in 1779 combined for protection. This
pioneer association was followed by the great fur-
trading companies, the Northwest and the Mackinaw
Company, the latter of which gained a strong hold
on Michigan trade. Two wars, a bitter competitive
feud among traders, a free policy of trade, and the
extension into its territory of the operations of two
great fur-trading companies mark the British régime.
It was largely through the influence of the latter, that
in spite of the fact that British power in United States
fell in 1783, and posts like Michilimackinac and Detroit
were evacuated in 1796, yet British influence in trade,

particularly in the region of Michilimackinac, prevailed until after the War of 1812.

A closer, more systematic organization of the trade
and a wholesale despoiling of the hunting grounds
characterized the American domination. This régime
saw the height of the Michigan fur trade and its
decline. Headed by the American Fur Company
located at Michilimackinac, organized armies of traders
with efficient leaders were sent into carefully mapped
out districts. Every hunting ground worth while had
its post. The company and independent traders
pushed trade hard until the forests began to yield a
poor return. There was no effort to preserve trade
but to get the most of it while it lasted.

The day of the fur trader is past, and any adequate
account of his operations in the various regions of the
Old Northwest and of the hardships of his life has
remained, practically, an unwritten chapter in our
nation's history. But surely, the influence of his
career on the life of the red men and the service he
rendered as a pathfinder are important enough for
civilization to entitle him to a unique place in the
story of Michigan.

TRADING POSTS OF THE FRENCH AND ENGLISH REGIMES
French ----●
English ---⚲

INDEPENDENT TRADING POSTS OF THE AMERICAN REGIME

LAKE SUPERIOR

Headquarters

LAKE MICHIGAN

LAKE HURON

Robinson's Fleet

Whitefish

Treaty posts with

SAGINAW BAY

Sloop

"Savage"

LAKE ST CLAIR

CANADA

LAKE ERIE

INDIANA   OHIO

TRADING POSTS OF THE AMERICAN FUR COMPANY

MICHIGAN LANDS CEDED BY INDIAN TREATIES

AMOUNT OF FUR IN MICHIGAN COUNTIES IN 1840

APPENDIX

APPENDIX

A sample of one of the Indian accounts taken from the Askin Blotter II:

Feb. 6, 1787.
Ash, a, wa, ha, may..........................Dr.
To Powder and Ball..............................
To 2 small blankets..............................
To tobacco and knife.............................
To 2 Beaver traps................................
To 5 Rolls worsted, 30 Raccoons..................
To 1 Blanket Strouds.............................
To 1 plain shirt 3 handkerchiefs & Fr. Box........

Pe, nis, e, ick, quay..........................Dr.
To 20 Bottles Rum................................

Achamit.......................................Dr.
To Powder and Ball, 5 Beavers...................

His first brother Dr. to powder and ball flints......

His second brother debtor to powder and ball......

Father to three, debtor to powder and ball..........

Ishcash.......................................Dr.
To 10 bottles rum................................

March 20, 1787.
Isbishsan......................................Dr.
To powder, ball, flints & knife...................

Mishas ....Dr.
To 3 pair of leggins, 1 knife......................
To sundries and 1 colored shirt...................
To one shirt and................................

Puck, cause................................Dr.
To powder and shot............................
To one deer skin...............................
To powder and lead............................

His sons...................................Dr.
To 2 fine shirts...............................

BIBLIOGRAPHY

BIBLIOGRAPHY

LETTERS, RECORDS, ACCOUNT BOOKS AND MANUSCRIPTS

JOHN ASKIN. (1) *Blotters and Ledgers.* These cover the period from 1788-1804. They show the nature of articles bought for Indian trade and the amount of furs brought to this one Detroit establishment. The occupation of each customer is given, hence, traders, engagés, etc. can be distinguished from others. In many cases the region where the trader is located is designated. Originals in *Burton Hist. Coll.*, Detroit; (2) *Diaries.* Of little value in the study of fur trade; (3) *Letters.* These cover the period, 1778-1810. They show the interference of war with the trade, also some of the operations of the North West Company and the names of traders, etc. They are found among the Askin Papers, *Burton Hist Coll.*, Detroit. A large number of them are published in the *Wis. Hist. Colls.*, XIX.

American Fur Company, *Account Books.* Most of the account books kept by the company at Mackinac are destroyed. In 1836 several boxes of these books were opened and the contents used for lighting fires, etc. Mrs. B. F. Felix of Chicago rescued several volumes, most of which were presented to the Chicago Historical Society, but the Society's collection was destroyed in the fire of 1871. Mrs. Felix kept one volume, from which extracts are given in the *Wis. Hist. Coll.*, XI. A few volumes are preserved in the Astor Hotel, Mackinac Island. Extracts from these are found in volume XII, of the *Wis. Hist. Colls.* Photostat copies are on file in the office of the Michigan Historical Commission, Lansing.

WILLIAM BURNETT. *Day Book and Blotter.* One blotter covers the period from April 3, 1796, to Oct. 4, 1797. Ledger "B" covers the period, 1791-1799, and the Day Book the period, 1799-1802. The former is in the possession of L. E. Merchant of St. Joseph, Michigan; the two latter, of the Northern Indiana Historical Society, South Bend, Indiana. Aside from showing the men engaged in the fur tradè at St. Joseph, Chicago and Milwaukee in those days and giving a fairly good idea of the kind and number of furs disposed of in this region, the books are interesting in themselves. The Blotter of 1796 is paper covered and all entries in it are made at St. Joseph and Michilimackinac. Ledger "B" is a thick leather bound volume, and the Day Book is paper covered like the Blotter, both evidently home made. Ledger "B" shows some ten accounts carried over from a Ledger "A," which has not been located. The watermark on the paper in the Day Book and Blotter has "Britania" in oval, surmounted by a crown. Ledger "B" has the royal arms surmounted by a crown with "G. R." below. All entries seem to be made by one person, evidently Wm. Burnett.

DOUGLAS BRYMNER. *Report on Canadian Archives.* Nineteen volumes, (1881-1906). This is of value in the study of the French and English fur-trading régimes.

HENRY BOUQUET. *Papers.* Extracts from his journals and letters are published in the *Mich. Hist. Colls.*, XIX, and cover the period, 1759-65.

ANTOINE DE LA MOTHE CADILLAC. *Papers.* These are translations from the original documents preserved in the archives of Paris, France. Papers dealing particularly with Detroit and Michigan history are published in the *Mich. Hist. Colls.*, XXXIII and XXXIV. A few of these are also found in the *New York Colonial Documents*, the *Wis. Hist. Colls.*, and in Sheldon's *History of Michigan.* Much material has been taken from them in this study.

RAMSAY CROOKS. *Letters.* These cover the period from Oct. 21, 1813, to July 28, 1830. Transcripts of the originals in the *Burton Hist. Coll.*, were used here. Several of these are published in the *Wis. Hist. Colls.*, XIX. They are of considerable value in studying the operations of the American Fur Company, the trade during the War of 1812, and the prices of furs.

Detroit *Gazette.* Copies of this paper from July 25, 1817, to June 26, 1827 are in the Public Library at Detroit. A few articles on the fur trade and quotations of market prices of furs may be found in them.

LIEUT. GOV. HALDIMAND. *Papers.* These are composed of transcripts of letters from and to Gov. Haldimand, memorandums and memorials sent to him; copies of papers on file in the Dominion Archives at Ottawa, Canada, pertaining to the relations of the British Government with the Indian tribes of North America, to the military posts, and to the marine interests of the Great Lakes (1762-1799). They are published in the *Mich. Hist. Colls.*, IX, X, XI, XIX, XX. Some are also found in the *Canadian Archives*, and the *Wis. Hist. Colls.* They have been of great value in the study of the English régime.

Laws of the North West Territory. Three volumes (1792-96). Vols. I and II were published in Philadelphia, III in Cincinnati. Copies in Law Library, University of Michigan.

WILLIAM JOHNSTON. *Letters on the Fur Trade 1833.* These are

published in the *Mich. Hist. Colls.*, XXXVII. They are edited
by J. S. Fox. He found them among the Schoolcraft papers
and the bundle bore the title, in Schoolcraft's handwriting,
"Manners and customs, Letters of *Miehgun*, an educated
grandson of Waubojeeg, the last ruler of the *Ojibway* dynasty
of Chegoimegon on Lake Superior." Wm. Johnston was the
son of John Johnston of Sault Ste. Marie. The letters are
addressed to his sister and cover the period from July 23 to
November 28, 1833. They give a vivid picture of the life of
a fur trader.

Jesuit Relations and Allied Documents. Travels and explorations
of the Jesuit missionaries in New France, edited by Reuben
Gold Thwaites, and published at Cleveland, 1896-1901.
Seventy-one volumes. Since the early French trader, as a
rule, was not a man of letters and left no accounts of his wanderings, we are forced to depend upon the missionary for a great
deal of our knowledge of the early French fur-trading régime.
Though much of the material here on the fur trade is of a general
nature, many facts have been gleaned from these pages for
this study.

L. R. MASSON. *Les Bourgeois de la Campagnie du Nord-Ouest.*
Quebec, 1889-90, two volumes. Volume I contains a short
account of the North West Company in French and a series
of letters and accounts of voyages relating to the North West
Canadian in English, also a list of the employees of the North
West Company in 1799 and 1804. Volume II is a continuation
of reports and letters. Among these is a letter of John Johnston,
trader at Sault Ste. Marie. It also contains a copy of the
agreements or constitutions of the North West Company for
1802 and 1804, Library of Congress. Volume II is in the
Burton Hist. Coll., Detroit.

New York Colonial Documents. Documents relative to the colonial
history of New York procured in Holland, England, and France
by John R. Brodhead, edited by E. B. O'Callaghan, Albany,
in ten volumes. Volumes IX (1855) and X (1858) of Paris
documents covering the periods 1631-1744 and 1745-1778,
respectively, have been used here in connection with the study
of the French régime. Some material has been taken from the
other volumes also.

JEAN BAPTISTE PERRAULT. *Narrative.* Travels and adventures
of a merchant voyageur in the savage territories of Northern
America leaving Montreal the 28th day of May, 1783 (to 1820),
edited by John Sharpless Fox. These are published in the
Mich. Hist. Colls., XXXVII. The narrative was found by
the editor among the Schoolcraft manuscripts in the Smithsonian
Institution at Washington. The narrative, says the editor,

was probably written from diaries kept by Perrault as indicated by the details given, such as exact dates, amount of merchandise with which he set out each year, number of packs and the prices at which he disposed of his furs. There are eleven maps showing the regions where he traveled. They throw an interesting light on the life of the fur trader.

Senate Documents. Some material on the American fur-trading régime is used here,—three volumes of the 22nd Congress. Washington, 1832.

American State Papers. Documents legislative and executive of the Congress of the United States. Vol. V, edited by Walter Lowrie and Walter S. Franklin, Washington, 1834, is used here. This deals with Indian affairs (1815-1827). Two volumes on navigation and commerce dealing with the periods 1789-1815 and 1815-23; the first edited by Walter Lowrie and Mathew St. Clair Clarke are also used. Both were published in Washington, 1832.

United States Statutes at Large. Public statutes at large of the United States of America, arranged in chronological order. Vols. I, II, III, were consulted for laws on trading houses and licenses. These three volumes were edited by Richard Peters, Boston, 1845-46.

United States Census Reports for 1840 and 1850 were used. They give the number of traders and the amount of fur in Michigan in those years.

Other blotters, records, and papers referred to: (1) Robert and James Abbott. *Papers.* Vol. 34, *Burton Hist. Coll.*, Detroit; (2) The J. J. B. account book, *Ibid;* (3) George Jacob, Ledger (1811-32). *Ibid;* (4) Michigan pamphlets, II, *Ibid;* (5) Rochedebault's memorandum book (1810-12), *Ibid;* (6) Sibley papers, *Ibid;* (7) Schoolcraft papers, *Ibid.* Some of these are in the *Mich. Hist. Colls.* (8) Williams papers, *Ibid;* (9) Woodbridge papers, *Ibid.*

Wisconsin Historical Collections. Though all of these are rich in material on the Northwest fur trade, volumes XVI, XVII, XVIII, and XIX have been of especial value, particularly volume XIX, the last half of which is entirely devoted to the fur trade. Beginning with volume XVI through volume XVIII are transcripts of documents made for the Wisconsin Historical Society from the *French Archives* in Paris, supplemented by documents already published in the *New York Colonial Documents*, Pièrre Margry's *Découvertes et Etablissements des Francais*, *Jesuit Relations*, La Pothier's *Histoire*, Charlevoix's *Histoire* and the *Canadian Archives*. These documents cover the period 1634-1800.

Michigan Historical Collections. Thirty-nine volumes. Aside from the papers already noted as found in these *Collections*, such as Haldimand, Cadillac papers, etc., many reminiscences, biographies, autobiographies of and papers on the Michigan fur traders, also estimates of the amount of fur and prices, are found and have been used.

Minnesota Historical Collections.

Illinois Historical Collections.

JOURNALS

PIERRE F. X. DE CHARLEVOIX. *Journal of a Voyage to North America.* Undertaken by order of the French king [etc.]. Contains a geographical description and general history of the country, particularly Canada, with an account of the customs, characters, religion, manners, and traditions of the original inhabitants in a series of letters translated from the French. Two volumes, London, 1761.

DANIEL WILLIAMS HARMON. *A Journal of Voyages and Travels in the Interior of North America* [etc.]. Edited by Daniel Haskel. New York, 1903.

ALEXANDER HENRY. *Travels and Adventures in Canada and the Indian Territories between the Years 1760 and 1776.* Printed and published by I. Riley. New York and Montreal, 1809.

LOUIS A. LA HONTAN. *New Voyages to North America.* Two volumes, edited by R. G. Thwaites, Chicago, 1905. Reprinted from the English edition of 1703.

HENRY R. SCHOOLCRAFT. *Narrative Journal of Travels ... from Detroit Through the Great Chain of American Lakes to the Sources of the Mississippi River*, [etc]. Albany, 1821.

Early Western Travels, 1748-1846. Edited by Reuben Gold Thwaites, in thirty volumes. Cleveland, 1904-06. These are a series of reprints of some of the best and rarest volumes of travel in the Middle and Far West during the period of early American settlement. Useful in studying the English and American régimes.

GENERAL WORKS USED

C. W. BUTTERFIELD. *History of the Discovery of the North West in 1634 by Jean Nicolet, With a Sketch of His Life.* Cincinnati, 1881.

HIRAM M. CHITTÉNDEN. *The American Fur Trade of the Far West* [etc.]. This is a history of the pioneer trading posts and the early fur companies of the Mississippi Valley and the Rocky Mountains, and the overland commerce with Santa Fé. New York, 1902. Has been used here in connection with the study of the life of the trader.

JOHN DUN. *History of the Oregon Territory and the British North American Fur Trade.* London, 1846. Of value in the study of the fur trade in general.

WASHINGTON IRVING. *Astoria, or Anecdotes of an Enterprise beyond the Rocky Mountains.* New York, 1882. This is a general account of the fur trade, method of trade, coureurs de bois and the North West, Mackinac and American Fur Companies. The appendix contains a few letters and petitions on the fur trade. A classic library account.

FRANCIS PARKMAN. *The Old Régime in Canada.* Boston, 1874; *Count Frontenac and New France under Louis XIV,* Boston, 1877; *Discovery of the Great West.* Boston, 1870; *Conspiracy of Pontiac.* Boston, 1868.

HENRY R. SCHOOLCRAFT. *Onéota, or Characteristics of the Red Race of America, from Original Notes and Manuscripts.* New York and London, 1845. This contains some autobiographical letters of John Johnston of Sault Ste. Marie.

P. F. X. CHARLEVOIX. *History and General Description of New France.* Six vols., trans. by J. G. Shea. New York, 1866-72.

THOS. L. McKENNEY. *Memoirs, Official and Personal with Sketches of Travels among the Northern and Southern Indians* [etc.]. New York, 1846.

BECKLES WILLSON. *The Great Company.* London, 1899. This was compiled from the company's archives, from diplomatic documents and state papers in France and England, from narratives of factors and traders, and from many accounts and memoirs.

JUSTIN WINSOR. *Narrative and Critical History of America.* 8 vols. Boston and New York, 1889. Volumes I, IV, VI, VII and VIII, contain a little material on the fur trade.

SPECIAL AND LOCAL HISTORIES OF MICHIGAN

THOS. COOLEY. *Michigan.* In American Commonwealths Series. Boston, 1889.

FRANKLIN EVERETT. *Memorials of the Grand River Valley.* Chicago, 1878.

SILAS FARMER. *The History of Detroit and Michigan* [etc.]. Detroit, 1884.

Michigan Biographies, Compiled by S. D. Bingham. The early history of Michigan, with biographies of State officers, members of Congress, etc. Lansing, 1888.

ROBT. B. ROSS. *History of the Knaggs Family* [etc.]. Detroit, 1902.

ROSS AND CATLIN. *Landmarks of Wayne County and Detroit.* Detroit, 1898.

E. M. SHELDON. *The Early History of Michigan from the First Settlement to 1815*. Detroit, 1856. This contains copies of manuscripts obtained from colonial archives in Paris, of which some use has been made.

CHAS. R. TUTTLE. *General History of the State of Michigan* [etc.]. Detroit, 1873.

UTLEY AND CUTCHEON. *Michigan as a Province, Territory and State* [etc.]. 4 vols. [New York], 1906.

American Biographical History of Eminent and Self-Made Men, with Portrait Illustrations on Steel, Michigan volume. Cincinnati, 1878. This is a compilation based upon information given by leading Michigan citizens.

County Histories: (1) Ionia—*History of Ionia, History and Directory of Ionia County* [etc.], compiled and published by J. D. Dillenbach, Grand Rapids, 1881; (2) Jackson—*History of Jackson County* [etc.], by the Interstate Pub. Co., Chicago, 1881; (3) Kalamazoo—*History of Kalamazoo County*, by Chas. C. Chapman & Co., Chicago, 1881; (4) Kent—*History and Directory of Kent County* [etc.], compiled and published by Dillenbach and Company, Grand Rapids, 1870; (5) Lapeer—*History of Lapeer County* [etc.], by H. R. Page & Co., Chicago, 1884; (6) Livingston—*History of Livingston County* [etc.], by Franklin Ellis, Philadelphia, 1880; (7) Macomb—*History of Macomb County* [etc.], by M. A. Leeson & Co., Chicago, 1882; (8) Montcalm—*History of Ionia and Montcalm Counties* [etc.], J. S. Schenck, Philadelphia, 1881; (9) Muskegon—*History of Muskegon County* [etc.], by H. R. Page & Co., Chicago, 1882; (10) Oakland—*History of Oakland County* [etc.], by W. Durant, Philadelphia, 1877; (11) Saginaw—*History of Saginaw County* [etc.], by Chas. C. Chapman & Co., Chicago, 1881; (12) St. Clair County, Michigan. *Its History and Its People* [etc.], by William Lee Jenks, 2 vols., Lewis Pub. Co., Chicago, 1912; *History of St. Clair County* [etc.], published by A. T. Andreas & Co., Chicago, 1883; (13) Washtenaw—*History of Washtenaw County* [etc.], published by Chas. Chapman & Co., Chicago, 1881.

MONOGRAPHS AND SHORT ARTICLES WRITTEN ON THE FUR TRADE

GEORGE A. BAKER. "Some Early Fur Traders of St. Joseph Valley." This is published in the *New Era*, a Northern Indiana Weekly. File in Library of Indiana Hist. Soc., South Bend, Indiana.

OTTO FOWLE. "Old Times in the Soo," published in the Sault Ste. Marie *Evening News* for Feb. 22, 1913.

F. F. GUNTHER. "The Fur Trade." This is published in Depew's

*History of American Commerce by One Hundred Americans,
1795-1895*, Vol. II. New York, 1895.
C. M. HARVEY. "Fur Traders as Empire-Builders," published
in the *Atlantic Monthly*, Vol. CIII.
REBECCA L. RICHMOND. "The Fur Traders of the Grand River
Valley," in *Publications*, Historical Society of Grand Rapids,
No. 3, Vol. I, Part 3. This gives a sketch of the life of Rix
Robinson, Louis and Antoine Campau, and Richard Godfroy.
BENJAMIN SULTE. "Le Commerce de France avec le Canada
avant 1760," in *Proceedings and Transactions*, Royal Society
of Canada, Second Series, XII, Part I.
FREDERICK J. TURNER. *The Character and Influence of the Indian
Trade in Wisconsin, a Study of the Trading Post as an Institution.*
Baltimore, 1891. In Johns Hopkins University Studies, ninth
series, XI-XII. A study of the trading post as an institution.
An excellent monograph on the fur trade. See also Wis. Hist.
Soc. *Proceedings*, 1889.

INDEX

INDEX

Abbott Bros., at Detroit, 94, 138, 144; Papers, 186

Accounts, of trade, 23, 104; sample of Indian, 181-182

Acts, relating to trading houses, 104-105

Agriculture, a minor factor, 7-8; discouraged, 76, 148-149

Algonquins, Nicolet visits, 6

American Fur Company, chartered, 110; during War of 1812, 122; organized, 123; traders, 124-125, 127-128; regions of trade, 125-126, 137-140; trading posts, 129, 142-145, 175; relation to independent trader, 137-138; sells out, 153; employees, 158; account books, 183

Amount of fur, difficulty in estimating, 23; beaver market, 30, 36-38, 39; at Detroit, 51, 72-73, 115, 144; at Michilimackinac, 59, 97, 115; during Revolutionary War, 95, 96-98; collected by Williams Bros., 139-140; in closing days of trade, 153; map showing fur in 1840, 177

Animals, furred, around Detroit, 3, 32, 36; in St. Joseph Valley, 3

Artisans, 158

Askin, John, at Michilimackinac, 82-84, 92-93; at Detroit, 93-94, 114; at Sault Ste. Marie, 95; mentioned, 101; Blotters and Ledgers, 93, 183

Association of traders, at Michilimackinac, 88-89; articles of agreement, 88-89

Astor Company, 92; gets interests of South West and North West

Companies, 123; see also American Fur Company

Astor, George, 119

Astor, John Jacob, 108; and Mackinaw Company, 110, 117; goes to Washington, 118; and Rix Robinson, 132; sells out, 144-145; see also American Fur Company

Baptiste, Charles J., 90

Barthe, Jean Baptiste, 82, 93

Bassett, Major Henry, on traders, 75, 159; refuses passes for St. Joseph Valley, 79

Beaver, market, 3, 23-24, 28, 29, 30, 35, 40, 43, 44, 51, 74, 98, 115; as rent, 4; suppressed, 36-37, 38

Beschefer, quotation from, 20

Bertrand, Joseph, 109, 143

Bibliography, 183-192

Boishébert, Sieur de, commandant at Detroit, 48

Bostwick, 73

Branford, Louis, 140

Buffalo fur, price, 37

Bourgeois, 155-156

Burnett, William, in St. Joseph Valley, 95, 99-100; in Grand River Valley, 108-109; and liquor traffic, 151, 160; Day Book and Blotter, 183-184

Cadillac, De La Mothe, and Jesuits, 14, 34; at Michilimackinac, 22; at Detroit, 32-43; under Company of Colony, 36; arrested, 38; in chief command at Detroit, 39; lures Indians to Detroit, 40-41, 52-53; policy of trade, 41, 43; and liquor traffic, 41; and illicit trade, 42-43; sent to Louisiana,

43; loses belongings, 44-;54
Papers, 184
Cadotte, J. B., 76
Cadotte, M., 71
Callières, Chev. de, 32
Campau, Antoine, 135-136, 138
Campau, George, 136
Campau Louis, 134-135; in Grand
    River Valley, 137-138; and
    Indians, 142
Campion, Etienne, 69
Canoe, and trade, 59, 81-82, 84
Carheil, Etienne, and trade, 13, 27,
    28; at Michilimackinac, 52-54;
    description of trader's life, 159-
    160
Céloron, Sieur de, at Detroit, 49
Champigny, M. de, illicit trade, 27,
    28-29; mentioned, 32
Champlain, Samuel, sends Nicolet
    westward, 6-7; at Saginaw, 8
Chappee, hut stolen, 141
Charlevoix, Pièrre de, 23, 62
Chippewas, greet Henry, 69-70; at
    Sault Ste. Marie, 71; visits
    "Williams' Exchange," 140
Chouart, Médard, at Sault Ste.
    Marie, 11
Clerk, 157
Commissioners for Trade and
    Plantations, 76
Company, colonizing, 4; Compagnie
    des Indes Occidentales, 4; of the
    Domain, 4, 35; of a Hundred
    Associates, 4; of the Colony, 5,
    33, 35-40, 42; origin of fur trad-
    ing, 65; North West, 82, 90-91,
    92, 93, 96, 107, 111, 119-121;
    Mackinaw, 89-90, 91-92, 107-108,
    110, 113, 117; General Company
    of Lake Superior region and the
    South, 90; XY, 91, 111-112;
    Astor, 92, 123; American Fur,
    110, 122-126, 127, 128, 137-138,
    142-145, 175, 183; Hudson Bay,
    132, 134, 151

County, St. Clair, 3, 95-96; Monroe,
    96; Menominee, 96, 141; Kent,
    130; Ionia, 130; Ottawa, 130;
    Mecosta, 141, Oakland, 141,
    Jackson, 141; Kalamazoo, 141;
    bibliography, 188, 189
Coureurs de bois, 5, 7, 8, 10-11, 14,
    16, 17, 19, 20, 21, 22, 26, 28, 54,
    61, 66, 72, 155
Crépieul, Jesuit and trade, 13
Crooks, Ramsay, at Michilimacki-
    nac, 118-119; over Northern De-
    partment, 123-124; buys out
    Northern Department, 145, 153;
    and factory system, 146; and De-
    troit trade, 152-153; Letters, 184

Detroit, key to upper-country
    trade, 3; fur bearing animals, 3,
    32; coureurs de bois, 8; Ft. St.
    Joseph on the Detroit, 20-21;
    illicit trade at, 42-43, 75; great
    depot of trade, 31-51; the found-
    ing of, 31-32; Company of Colony
    and, 35-39; Cadillac chief at, 39-
    43; restrictions on trade, 40;
    various masters, 44-49; trade
    farmed out, 46; conditions of
    trade at, 49-50, 93-94, 97, 115,
    121, 144; British at, 49, 68; war
    and trade at, 74-75, 79, 80, 85,
    121-122; John Askin at, 92-93;
    Yankee enters, 108, 121; Ameri-
    can régime at, 143-144; decline
    of trade, 152-153
Dubuisson, M., takes Cadillac's
    goods, 44-45
DuLhut, Daniel Greyselon, tem-
    porary trading post, 10; post at
    Detroit, 20
Durantaye, La, 19, 20, 21
D'Aigremont, M., inspects western
    posts, 42-43, 54, 55
Dease, John, 80
Denonville, sends DuLhut to De-
    troit, 20; control of trade, 21

De Noyan, at Detroit, 48-49
Departments of trade, organized, 123; Northern, 123-126, 145, 153; Western, 145
DeQuindre, clerk for American Fur Company, 138
Desnoyers, Baptiste, 140

Engagés, 158, 167
English traders, and Indians, 17, 57, 61, 66, 67, 73, 80; and French, 49, 63; killed, 73; elimination of, 100-101, 106, 114; becomes American subjects, 107; and smuggling, 112, 113; grievances, 113
Emalinger, Charles, 120
Etherington, George, 68

Factory system, established, 102-105; new factories, 109-110; in St. Joseph Valley, 109; Crooks opposes, 146; abolished, 146; causes of failure, 147
Fairs, at Montreal and Three Rivers, 5
Farley, interpreter, 69, 71
Farnsworth, and Brush steal a trading hut, 141
Firms, trading, 83, 87, 89, 91, 93-94, 111, 112, 119, 135-136; at Detroit, 143-144
Flemings, and British at Michilimackinac, 18-19
Forest, Sir de la, 34; at Detroit, 44-45
Forsyth, Robert, 95
Framboise, Joseph la, and Grand River Valley, 96, 129, 130; Madame la, 108, 130-131, 133
Frobisher, Benjamin, 90
Frontenac, Count, and liquor traffic, 26
Ft. Joseph on the Detroit, 30

Gage, General Thomas, 66, 69
Gazette, Detroit, 144, 146, 149, 184
Genereaux, Louis, 136

George III, 64
Goddard, Stanley, 70
Godfroy, family of traders, 136
Godfroy, Richard, steamboat on Grand River, 136; in Saginaw Valley, 140
Grand Portage, 82, 83, 91, 92, 94
Grand River Valley, under Michilimackinac, 59-60; Langlade takes command of, 60; Framboise, Monsieur and Madame, in, 96, 108, 129-131, 133; Burnett in, 108-109; American Fur Company in, 129-137; Campau, Louis, in, 137-138
Grant, Charles, 81
Greeley, Horace, quotation, 148
Groseilliers, Sieur de, at Sault Ste. Marie, 11, 14
"Griffin," La Salle's, 11-12, 82

Haldimand, Lieutenant Governor, 75, 82, 84, 184
Hambach, J. D., 71
Hamilton, Lieutenant Governor, 84, 85
Hennepin, Father Louis, 11
Henry, Alexander, at Michilimackinac, 68-74; mentioned, 162
Hivernans, 158
Howard, Captain, 74
Hubbard, G. S., 131
Hubbel, J. B., buys out American Fur Company, 153
Hudson Bay, English post at, 17
Hudson Bay Company, and American Fur Company, 132, 134; smuggling liquor, 151
"Hunter, General," the sloop, 151

Illicit trade, universal, 27; at Detroit, 42-43, 47, 75; at Michilimackinac, 27-30, 53, 54-55
Indians, Iroquois, 2, 18-19, 20, 21, 22, 31, 32, 33, 41, 43, 62; Algonquins, 6; Nipissings, 6; Dacotahs,

7; Winnebagos, 7; Hurons, 7, 18, 19, 40, 47, 48, 52-53, 75; at Sault Ste. Marie, 15; Saulteurs, 15, 57; Potawatomi, 15, 23, 40, 62, 75; British and, 17, 57, 61, 66, 67, 72, 73, 80; Lupes, 18; Misusokis, 18; Ottawas, 18, 19, 20, 40, 48, 52, 55, 57, 70, 75, 152; Sioux, 20; Baie des Puants, 20; Illinois, 20, 29; Miamis, 20, 29, 34, 62, 93; French and, 57, 66, 67; see also coureurs de bois; Chippewas, 69-70, 71, 75, 140; and Yankees, 114, 134, 139, 141-142; Menominee, 141; and settlers, 150; art of story telling, 164

Iroquois, see Indians

Irwin, Mathew, 148

Jay's treaty, 107

Jesuit, life, 9, 10, 12; relation to trade, 12-14, 51; influence and service, 12-13, 17, 28; and Cadillac, 14, 34, 52; at Sault Ste. Marie, 16; and liquor traffic, 25-26

Jewett, Eleazer, at Saginaw, 137

Johnston, John, at Sault Ste. Marie, 112, 120-123; in service of American Fur Company, 123, 142-143

Johnston, William, 128, 184

Jogues, Isaac, at Sault Ste. Marie, 15

Kinzie, John, 95, 100

Knaggs, Whitmore, 140

La Durantaye, chases Flemings and British, 19; takes possession of region around Detroit, 20-21; western traders and, 21

La Salle, Robert de, 11-12

Laval, Bishop, and liquor traffic, 25-26

Le Jeune, 9, 13, 162

Leslie, Lieutenant, 71

Le Claire, Andrew, 95

LeClaire, Antoine, 95

Langlade, 129

Licenses, beginning of, 6; at Detroit, 47, 48; cheap, 50; restored, 46, 55-56, 57; during war, 58-59; penalty for trading without, 65; under British régime, 64-65; under United States régime, 105-106; opposition to, 147-148; misuse of, 148; and liquor traffic, 151

Liquor traffic, rum, 19; problem of, 25; and Indian, 24, 25, 50; attempts to stop, 25-27, 44, 56, 86; Cadillac and, 41, Tonty and, 47; at Michilimackinac, 53, 54, 56, 86-87; smuggling in, 54, 86-87, 151; and English, 41, 62; and factory, 103; and individual trader, 147; under American régime, 151-152; and early settlers, 152; and Burnett, 151, 160

Long, John, 76

Louis XIV, 26, 29

Louvigny, Monsieur M., 55, 56

Lusson, Monsieur de Saint, claims region around Sault Ste. Marie for the French, 16

Lyed-corn, how prepared, 162

Mackinaw Company, origin, 89-90; composition and region of trade, 91-92; influence, 107-108; Astor buys share in, 110; convoy of, 113

Mackenzie, Alexander, 94

Mangeurs-de-lard, 157, 167

Maps, French and English trading posts, 173; independent posts, 174; American Fur Company's posts, 175; territory ceded by Indians, 176; amount of fur in 1840, 177

Marquette, Father, establishes mission, 16

May, James, 100

McDonald, William, at Saginaw, 137

McGill, James, 107
McGregor, and Rooseboom lead expedition against Michilimackinac, 18
Michigan, advantages in trade, 1-3; first traders in, 11; first mission in, 15
Michilimackinac, location for trade, 3, 16-17; pioneer traders, 16; Flemings and British attack, 18-19; Intercolonial Wars and, 22, 58; illicit trade at, 27-30, 53, 54-55; re-establishment of, 43, 58; Indians lured away from, 52-53; liquor traffic at, 53, 54, 56; amount of fur at, 59, 97, 115; under English control, 68; Pontiac's War and, 73-74; abandoned, 74; visit of trading canoes, 81-82; Revolutionary War and, 80, 83-84; traders' union, 88-90; under United States régime, 107-108; factory at, 109; War of 1812 and, 117-119; American Fur Company at, 123-124, 126, 144, 153; a traders' rendezvous, 164-165

Niagara, 21
Nicknames, of traders, 135, 136
Nicolet, Jean, tour westward, 6-8, importance, 14; at Michilimackinac, 16
Northern Department, organized, 123-126; Crooks buys, 145, 153
North Westers, 81, 96, 122-123, 134
Nouvel, Father, 17-18
North West Company, builds vessel for trade, 82; organized, 90-91; at Grand Portage, 92; and Detroit, 93-94; at Sault Ste. Marie, 95; post of, 96; maintains English influence, 107; canal at Sault Ste. Marie, 111; during War of 1812, 119-121

"Opposition," and trading companies, 127-128, 129; Rix Robinson and, 132-133, 134; in Saginaw Valley, 137-138; treatment of, 138, 141, 161, 171
Ottawas, and Iroquois, 18, 19; and English, 19, 20, 57, 70, 75; clash with Hurons, 48; attack Renards, 55; at Michilimackinac, 57, 70; and liquor traffic, 152
Outfits, trading, 168
"Outward invoices," of American Fur Company, 124-125, 131, 143

Partisan, 156
Perrault, Jean Baptiste, 89, 90, 162, 185
Peyster, Major de, 84, 88
Pierre, Mr. de St., 58
Policy, of trade, French, 4-6, 37-38, 40, 42, 50-51, 59-60, 61, 169-170; Cadillac's, 41, 43; British, 64-67, 171; French and British contrasted, 66-67; of United States, 102-106, 123, 146-147, 172; of American Fur Company, 124; of Yankee, 136-137
Pontchartrain, Count, and Cadillac, 32, 37; complaints by Company of Colony to, 39
Population of Michigan, 149
Pork eaters, 157, 167 .
Portages, method of crossing, 166-167
Posts, on Mississippi, 2; on Hudson Bay, 5; French, 10-11, 15, 22, 30, 63, 170, 173; English, 17, 66, 91, 95-96, 107, 173; western, 21, 42-43, 55, 66, 68, 111; northern, 59, 60; of Williams' Bros., 138-139; interior abandoned, 153; American, 101, 140-141, 142-144; of American Fur Company, 129, 142-145, 175
Potawatomi, flee, 15; in St. Joseph Valley, 23; at Detroit, 40; region of trade, 62; confiscates liquor, 151

Presents, and Iroquois, 18; and British, 18, 61, 65-66, 147; and French, 33, 62; and Indians, 54, 62, 65, 69-70; use of by "Opposition," 128; and Indian agents, 147

Price of fur, fixing of, 23-24, 75, 101, 103; falling of, 28, 114-115; of buffalo, 37; at Detroit, 48-49, 50,. 121-122; quotations of, 116; Indian's estimate of, 160; British and French, 170

Puthuff, Major, and license system, 148

Radisson, Pièrre, 11, 14

Raymbault, Charles, at Sault Ste. Marie, 15

Réaume, trouble with independent trader, 137-138

Recollect, John Baptiste, post in Muskegon, 136

Régime, French, 4-63, 169-170; British, 64-101, 170-172; American 102-153, 172

Regulations of trade, 16, 28, 55-56, 60-61, 112

Riverin's report of the Company of Colony, 38-39

Roberts, Charles, seizes Michilimackinac, 117

Robertson, Samuel, 82, 93

Robinson, Rix, manager of American Fur Company, 129-130; in Grand River Valley, 131-135; relation to Indians, 141; gives up trade, 146, education, 160

Rocheblave, Mr. de, 86

Rogers, Captain Roberts, 68

Routes of trade, 1-2, 3, 16, 23

Sabrevois, M. de, at Detroit, 45-46

Saginaw, Champlain and, 8, "Opposition" in, 137; American Fur Company in, 137-140

Saulteurs, 15, 39

Sault Ste. Marie, importance of location of, 3; early traders, 8, 11,

15-16; mission, 15-16; Indians at, 15; abandoned, 30, 73; re-established, 60-61; in 1762, 71; in 1765, 76; trading canoes at, 81-82; during the Revolutionary War, 95; North West Company at, 95, 111-112; during War of 1812, 119-121; John Johnston at, 119-123; American Fur Company at, 142-143

Sayer, John, with Burnett, 99

Settlement, Lord Commissioners for Trade and Plantations on, 76, 148; inroad on trade, 37-38, 106, 153; French and English attitude toward, 148-149; attitude of Yankee, 149; Indian and, 150

"Shiawassee Exchange," 140

Simcoe, Governor J. G., 79

Smuggling, of liquor, 54, 86-87, 151; British, 112, 113

Solomons, Ezekiel, 70, 73, 88

St. Joseph Island, British trading post at, 107; captured, 119

St. Joseph Valley, fur bearing animals in, 3; favorite trading route, 23; during French régime, 11-12, 61-62; in 1762, 71; Pontiac's War, 73; passes for, 79; Michilimackinac Association and, 89; LeClaire in, 95; Burnett in, 95, 99-100, 151; during Revolution, 95; furs handled in, 97; American influence in, 109; American Fur Company and, 143

Stuart, Robert, in the service of American Fur Company, 123-124, 133, 144-145

Suay, Leon, 140

Sulte, 7

Summary, 169-172

Systems, of trade, license, 6, 46, 47, 55-56; farming out trade, 46, 62; factory, 102-104

Tonty, Sieur Alphonse de, at Mich-

ilimackinac, 29; plans post among
Miamis, 34; at Detroit, 46-48
Tonty, Henry de, 11
Tonty, M. de, 42
Trade, pioneer, 1-30; competition
in, 17, 78, 80, 87, 92, 124-125,
127-128, 137-138; protection of,
17; war and, 21-22, 50, 55, 58-59,
62, 73, 74, 78-101, 95, 96-98, 106,
114, 117-126; goods exchanged in,
72-73, 103, 126; at its height, 127-
145; method of, 143, 147, 165-
166, 167-169; decline of, 146, 150,
152-153, 169
Traders, and Indians, 5, 17, 57, 58,
61, 66, 67, 73, 80, 134, 141-142,
146; character, 8, 75, 159-162;
first in Michigan, 11; life of, 12,
133, 154-172; English, 30, 49, 72,
76, 106, 107, 110, 113, 114, 123,
127, 170; independent, 50-51,
127-128, 134-135, 140, 143, 158,
168-169; French, see coureurs de
bois; contests among, 65, 78, 87,
127-128, 132-133, 134, 137, 161;
Yankee, 78-79, 99, 100-101, 108-
109, 114, 127; union among, 88-
90; relation to companies, 92, 124-
125, 127-128, 129, 137-138; women, 130-131, 139; classes of,
155-158, education of, 160-161;
food, 162-163; recreation, 163-

165; physical examination of, 159;
service of, 161
Transportation, the "Griffin," 11-
12, 82; during the Revolutionary
War, 81-85; private trading
vessel, 82-83, 91; during War of
1812, 118-119; fleet on Grand
River, 133-134, 136; schooner,
"Union," 119; the sloop, "Sav-
age," 139; the sloop, "General
Hunter," 82, 151; cost of, 168
Treaties, with Indians, 150, 176
Turner, Frederick, 3, 10, 13

Varnum, Joseph B., 109
Vaudreuil, Governor, 56
Vimont, Father, and fur trade, 13-
14
Voyageurs, 60, 81-82, 156-157

War, Intercolonial, 21-22, 50, 55,
58-59, 62, 171; Pontiac's, 73-74;
Revolutionary, 78-102; of 1812,
106, 114, 117-123; among traders,
17, 78, 85-86, 87-88, 92, 100
Williams, B. O. and A. L., tradin3
section of, 140; "Williams Exchange," 140
Williams, Ephraim and Gardiner,
138-140, 160, 164

XY Company, origin, 91; and North
West Company, 111-112